CHAMBER WORLD

*Insider Secrets to
Chambers of Commerce*

Patrick H. McGaughey, IOM, CPF

Creative Space, LLC * Virginia * United States

Published by: Creative Space, LLC Copyright

© 2024 by Patrick H. McGaughey

Published in the United States by Creative Space, LLC, 5810 Kingstowne Center Dr., Ste 120, PMB 286, Alexandria, VA 22315.

https://creativespacellcva.com

First Creative Space, LLC Edition 2024

Cover Art by Lory Mitchell Wingate.

All rights reserved. No part of this publication may be re-produced in any form, or by any means, electronic or mechanical, including photocopying, recording, or any information browsing, storage, or retrieval system, without permission in writing from the publisher.

Library of Congress Cataloguing-in-Publication Data: McGaughey, Patrick H.

Title of the Book: Chamber World | Insider Secrets to Chamber of Commerce Management

ISBN: 9798335249935
1- Chamber. 2- Commerce. 3- Nonprofit. 4-Business. 5- Leadership. 6- Management. 7- Membership. I. Chamber World | Insider Secrets to Chambers of Commerce

Author's Note

This book delves into real-life experiences of the author. The author acknowledges no liability for legal consequences arising from the reader's interpretation or application of the book's information. It's important to note that the book is meant solely for educational purposes.

This book is dedicated to my wife Gail, who is as marvelous as she is maddening and as inspiring as she is challenging. I have flown at 30,000 feet throughout my entire career, and it has been Gail in the control tower bringing me back down to earth day after day and time after time. I married up.

Preface

Most of us didn't grow up dreaming of being a chamber of commerce executive or chief executive officer. Nor did any of us grow up dreaming of working for, or for that matter, serving as a volunteer for, a chamber of commerce. I believe it's safe to say most of us arrived here accidentally and therefore we can be categorized as accidental executives, employees, volunteers, or board members.

Here's the point, we all remain accidental until we become intentional in industries we never dreamed of entering. What does this mean? If you grew up under a proud parent who was the president and chief executive officer of a chamber of commerce, you may have said, "I want to be like her." That's intentional.

My parents were both in medicine, and I wanted to be a broadcaster with no idea what a chamber was or what they did. I was truly an accidental chamber executive.

As a young adult, I did become a broadcaster and as a morning man in radio, I was a champion of my community getting my radio station behind popular civic campaigns and becoming the default leader, or at the very least, the figurehead of different campaigns.

You might say I was becoming a chamber executive, by accident.

I thrived on serving my community. I served as president of the Lion's Club and the local Little League and loved every minute of it. As if that wasn't enough, Gail and I combined our entrepreneurial spirits and started a music store as downtown merchants, and that's where we were introduced to the world of chambers of commerce, and it wasn't a positive experience.

Four local businessmen came in and were assertive in their quest that we join. They made it sound like it was a rule but promised us more customers and a better business environment. I paid up and never saw them again. They did send me twelve unreadable newsletters followed by an invoice to do it all over again a year later. I dropped that membership like a bad habit. It didn't start well.

Two years later, the local newspaper publisher who was coming in as the new Board Chairman of the Chamber, walked into our store and said, "Pat, you're going to be the new Executive Director of the Chamber of Commerce."

For context, I was still on the air at the radio station from 6:00 a.m. to 10:00 a.m. and then worked selling and producing radio commercials until 3:00 p.m. each day, Monday through Friday. Gail would manage the music store until I would show up in the afternoon to work until the 7:00 p.m. closing time and, we kept the store open seven days a week. We were young.

"Why would I want that job?" I asked the publisher, "To start with, he said, we're going to pay you more money." I said, "Keep talking." He said we're going to give you weekends off, and we're going to give you better benefits.

If you have any history inside the *Chamber World*, you know I had just been lied to three times, but I know he didn't know it. He and the Board did not know the true financial situation, or they were like many boards before and since, in denial of their poor financial status.

He also didn't realize being a chamber executive was a 24/7 job. Chamber executives can't go out to dinner or to the grocery store without being stopped to talk shop. We live, breathe, sleep and dream about our job, maybe not at first, but once we become intentional, it quickly impacts every part of our life, every day.

The publisher and I had a unique relationship. We were friends while being fierce competitors on the street fighting for advertising budgets and we were both equally fierce about the success of our small hamlet of The Dalles, Oregon. If anything, we trusted each other so we never put each other down because as competitors, we both knew that would be putting down advertising. We always took the high road in competing with each other.

I finally said, "Steve, that all sounds great, but you have to answer one question before I can decide." "Ask away" he said, and I did; "What do you people do? I was a member and still have no idea what goes on down there."

He smiled and said, "Pat, we do three things," and went on to explain. Afterwards I replied, "If I'd have known that I'd still be a member today!" "And THAT," he said, "is why you're going to be the next chamber executive. I know you can sell it!"

(Secret) What were the three things? First, he said, "The chamber is the local business and visitor *information center.*" For this alone he added, every business doing business in every community should support their local information center through a chamber membership.

"And as you boys in radio like to say, 'but wait, there's still more!' The Chamber is the local business *issue center*." He went on, "We work on issues that impact every cash register and every business budget every time there is an issue impacting the local business community."

"But the third reason will surprise you because it flies in the face of what you and I do every day."

"OK, surprise me," I said.

"Dollar for dollar, Pat, the chamber of commerce is a *marketing center* and the best marketing buy a business can make, simply through the networking and connections we all form by working our memberships."

It was at that moment, I understood why Steve Bennett was a far better salesperson than I was. Great salespeople sell in threes. The chamber is the information center, issue center and marketing center for local business. Sure, there's more, but this is all that's needed to instantly frame the value of any chamber, and why I use the perfect universal mission statement of *"We serve, protect, and promote our members"* as the starting point in explaining our world in my role as a consultant to our industry and as the author of this book.

I believe I was recruited by accident, but after Steve's explanation I jumped at the chance to lead The Dalles Area Chamber of Commerce as a fully intentional chamber executive. Now, as a veteran 'insider' of our industry, it's my goal to be an intentional author for sharing favorite lessons learned, as they became *secrets* to my success, inside the *Chamber World*.

I haven't changed a word of Steve Bennett's concise description of what every chamber of commerce does in my many years of serving, protecting, and promoting local businesses in Oregon, Washington, and beautiful Coeur d'Alene, Idaho.

- Patrick McGaughey

CHAMBER WORLD

*Insider Secrets to
Chambers of Commerce*

- Introduction v
- Telling Our Story 1
  - Major Players First 5
  - Humanizing Our Marketing Approach 10
  - Leveraging Technology 21
- Selling Our Story 31
  - Selling Memberships 35
  - Selling Sponsorships 52
- Engaging Volunteers 61
  - The Essence of Belonging 65
  - Aim Them in the Right Direction 74
  - Engaging Active Participation 85
- Let's Talk Money 99
  - Monetizing Our Value 102
  - Building a Pre-Approved Chamber Budget ... 113
  - Opportunities for Growing Money 121
- Playing By the Rules 125
  - The Legal Compass 128
  - The Alchemy of Board Composition 133
  - Shaping Boardroom Culture 142
- From Vision to Vitality 149
  - Branding Strategy and Mission Statement ... 152
  - Adaptation and Innovation 168
  - Operationalizing the Vision and Mission 178
- The Good Leader 181
  - Influence and Presence 184
  - Leading Through Wisdom Found 198
- Cultivating Excellence in Staff 221
  - Taking Care of Our People 226
  - If it's to be, it's NOT up to me. 228
  - The Secret to Motivating Others 230
  - For The Success of Others 232
- About the Author 235

Introduction

Let's get real as we enter *Chamber World* with a little pragmatism and this description of the chamber of commerce; it is the most POWERFUL, powerless organization ever created. Here's the reality, we are powerless because we are granted almost no authority. We can pass no law or establish any regulation. We can impose no tax or fee. The only official power a chamber of commerce has evidently, is that we can certify *Certificates of Origin*. How that came about is still a mystery.

Now you ask, how can we be the most powerful organization ever created if we're so powerless? The answer my friends, is the *secret* to our value. If we do our job well, the chamber of commerce can influence the passage or defeat of any law or regulation. We can influence the passage or defeat of any tax or fee, we just need to recognize and utilize the power we do have or should have.

Two things make a chamber of commerce powerful; the number of members we have and the amount of money we have. Our influence is dependent on the size of our membership and the size of our bank accounts. Money talks. We've all heard that cliché a million times and that's because nothing becomes a cliché unless it is fundamentally true. The size of our bank account allows us to back up our positions so we can put our money where our mouth is. Again, another cliché which remains equally true.

Now we come to the fundamental reason why every business in every community should be a card-carrying member of their local chamber of commerce. Power. You're more than a member when you join, you become a business constituent. Together, our members are the business constituency of every community with an active chamber of commerce. To elected officials, constituency means votes and votes are the currency of elected officials and therein lies our power. Anytime we can replace the words membership or member with constituent or constituency we are reminding our elected officials of the power we have and when we do, we'll have earned our seat at the table.

This is the heart of our *Chamber World*, but sadly, many don't recognize it and if we do recognize it, we often don't know how to build upon it. This book was designed to help executives, staff, board members, and volunteers build and establish more power for the business community within our individual *Chamber Worlds*.

This book is an offering of insights for executives, staff members, board members, committee members, and for general business members who are serious about the value of their chamber. They come from someone who entered the *Chamber World* as a downtown business member, who then dropped out after twelve months and was later recruited to the same chamber as its executive officer.

Readers can expect real world, pragmatic insights into the workings of a successful chamber of commerce with lessons in success and failure. Some will take inspiration while others will use this book for reference. There's an industry axiom that says, "If you've seen one chamber, you've seen one chamber," and that's true to a point, but others suggest an older axiom is more definitive; everything is different, but everything remains the same.

It is the mission of this book to stimulate innovative and productive thinking from the tried-and-true insights and experiences presented, while recognizing it all becomes dated material the moment it's printed. Many of the experiences are timeless and others, while ideal, or at least politically correct for their time, will hopefully generate new ideas and new thinking that fit today's needs.

Now enter *Chamber World,* an enlightening journey through a multifaceted landscape. And while it may lack the peaks and valleys of a historical exploration, navigating through board meetings and membership strategies promises its own brand of excitement. Fear not, for I am committed to infusing just the right amount of engagement to keep your attention.

We will explore Memberships – above and beyond becoming an exclusive club where networking opportunities abound. We'll uncover marketing strategies to attract, activate, and advance memberships to make the sales. We will also investigate ways to maintain member engagement, including the allure of enticing perks.

Moving forward, operating the chamber demands our attention – encompassing financial stewardship, technological integration, and establishing operational guidelines for stability within the chaos and uncertainty.

In the *Chamber World* geography, governance is the bedrock. Comparable to orchestrating a group of unruly cats, managing governance requires finesse. We'll delve into the legal roadblocks, navigating the nuances of diverse board politics, and ensuring alignment among stakeholders. Think of it as a comprehensive primer in the art of adulting for chamber executives and their volunteers.

Strategic planning may sound daunting, but it's simply about charting a course for success while avoiding potential pitfalls. We'll discuss effective goal setting and execution to ensure smooth sailing for your chamber.

Finally, leadership awaits – where true effectiveness transcends mere authority. We'll delve into the essential qualities of successful leadership, emphasizing active listening and establishing cohesion within the workplace.

While this whirlwind tour of our *Chamber World* may not match the thrills of a movie binge or weekend getaway, the knowledge gained promises to be transformative for you and your chamber. If this or any book excites you to the point of wanting to share copies with others, don't hold them hostage by asking them to read the entire book just because you bought it for them. Gift the book and pick just one chapter that excites you the most and ask them to read it. If a book is as good as we say, one great chapter will lead to another.

Let's embark on this invigorating journey through the captivating and often chaotic realm of chambers of commerce. By sharing the lessons lived and *secrets* found throughout my career, I wish to impart any wisdom I may have gained with you for use in your *Chamber World*.

Chapter One

Telling Our Story

CHAMBER WORLD

TELLING OUR STORY

A chamber of commerce is more than an organization; it's a nexus of power and purpose. When a business joins, they become a vital part of a dynamic membership constituency, a force to be reckoned with. Its collective voice resonates as it influences, shaping policies, driving change, and championing the interests of business and by default, the interests of our communities.

But let's strip away the illusions and repeat the raw reality: The chamber of commerce is paradoxically the most powerful, yet powerless organization ever created. Though it may lack any formal authority, its potential for influence is boundless when our membership is substantial. The volume in numbers and financial contributions are the keys to boosting the chamber's ability to advocate for business and the communities we serve, thus becoming more and more powerful.

Membership in the chamber should be positioned as a direct investment in our communities, tapping into the corporate and business psyche of civic responsibilities. In our unity lies our strength, and within our empowerment lies the promise of achieving things together that cannot be done alone.

The more businesses with their name on the rolls of the chamber, the more the collective voice of business will be heard. Influence and power grow exponentially as our numbers increase. A strong membership base equals a strong voice, powerful advocacy, and considerable impact on policymaking and community issues.

But why charge so much? Businesses, both large and small, are expensive to operate. Potential members must understand, and long-term members must remember that we are operating a business, not a club. All the operational costs of doing business that they have, we have. We are a private 501(C)6 non-profit business organization. We are a private business with a not-for-profit tax exemption. Non-profit is a tax status, not a business plan. The money we require is what keeps our lights on and our work moving forward at the highest possible level. We're running a business, just like them.

TELLING OUR STORY

Major Players First

Chambers of commerce should prioritize appealing to the largest businesses first and foremost in their marketing strategy for both organization growth and advocacy strength. Big business doesn't follow small business, but small businesses want to align themselves with big business. Small businesses learn and sometimes earn more from big business rather than the other way around in *Chamber World*. It is important to keep in mind that major players are a marketing magnet in attracting smaller businesses, so start with the courage, confidence, and competency that will attract major players and corporations.

Securing the membership and support of major players and prominent businesses not only builds the chamber's strength, credibility, and prestige, it also creates a strong foundation of stability through the substantial membership fees and sponsorship opportunities that major players bring to the table.

The problem lies in defining what we can do for them. *(Secret)* The great paradox in our industry is that big business thinks the local chamber of commerce is a small business organization while small businesses think we're a big business organization. It seems we can't win, but that's only true if we give up. When we hear these comments it's an excellent opportunity to show and prove the benefit of both classifications when big and small businesses work together to strengthen the power of the local business community.

Two things make a chamber of commerce powerful: money and members. Big business provides the money and prestige while small businesses provide the numbers for a larger constituency.

Pause and consider that for a moment. We don't use the word *constituency* enough. To be the voice of business, its constituency that means votes and votes are the currency of elected officials. *(Secret)* When sitting at the tables of government, don't use the term "our members" when you can always be more effective by saying "our constituency."

Discounting Our Price, Discounts Our Value

Before going further on marketing to major players remember this, never ever go on the cheap and think a low price is attractive to them. Cheap prices equate to cheap products and cut-rate services; it's not the image you want to sell and not the image major players want to buy. Put a price tag on membership and sponsorship levels that will get their

TELLING OUR STORY

attention. Serious issues require serious money, so get serious about pricing, especially with the major players in your *Chamber World*.

Major player involvement gives accountability and prestige to the chamber and will continue to attract smaller enterprises who seek the association and possible future partnerships with larger industry leaders. Smaller businesses and individual entrepreneurs want to become players and therefore want to be where the major players are.

With the major players in the game first, smaller businesses will expect their financial contribution will move up to be commensurate with the growing power and prestige of your growing chamber of commerce.

No matter the price, whether it's high or low, major, and minor players will both object at some level. Why? Because it's the nature of being a businessperson. It was Sam Walton who proved the importance of controlling business expenses, so be prepared to defend your serious pricing structure, and never apologize for keeping the lights on and people working to move the important issues forward.

Everyone has the same maintenance and operations expenses that we have, so remind them without apology and get back to the issues at hand because that's what they're paying for, successful issue management.

As the saying goes, money talks, and in our context, it speaks volumes. Money *amplifies* the chamber's voice, or bark if you will, and therefore turns up the volume of our advocacy efforts and solidifies our image as the watch dog and voice for business members and therefore the economic voice of our communities.

Opening Doors by Invitation

So how do we market most effectively to the major players? When looking for major players to recruit, try leveraging the chamber's board of directors to extend *personal invitations* to prospective members. This personalizes the approach of adding a board member's name to the invitation and increases the likelihood of a positive response. *(Secret)* This strategy only works if board members know that the invitation will not impact their personal or business relationships with these prospective members.

Start by showing board members the script to be used with every invitation.

"Mrs. Jones, Bob Smith who is on the Chamber Board asked me to personally invite you to be

TELLING OUR STORY

a member of the MyTown Chamber of Commerce. However, as Membership Director of the Chamber, I know that membership isn't right for everyone so I would like to set an appointment this week or next week, to review and see if membership is right for you."

What just happened? First, board member Bob finally put his name on a membership invitation (referral) because it wasn't a hard sell on his friend or colleague. Second, he doesn't have to do any work other than offer 12 names (one name per month) for an "invitation to join." Third, Mrs. Jones won't resent Bob for having the Chamber call with a gentle invitation that won't shame her or offend Bob if she doesn't join.

People love an invitation. If we utilize board members to warm up our cold calls like the example above, we will open more doors. When Mrs. Jones does join, post her picture side by side with Board member Bob's picture with a simple caption, "Mary Jones, Jones Insurance invited by Bob Smith, Smith Auto Group." (Mary improves her relationship with Bob, the Chamber gets the money and Bob along with his company get the credit.)

With this strategy, it's harder for Mrs. Jones to say no and even harder for her to drop later knowing she accepted Board member Bob's invitation. For Board member Bob, invitations are a low-risk way to encourage his vendors, customers, and colleagues, all without doing any of the sales work. If 15 board members give us 12 names per year, that's 180 warm invitations keeping our membership directors busy. Even if only 50% of those invitations join, the math says we'll have 90 new members in our *Chamber World* every year.

Humanizing Our Marketing Approach

Nothing influences the chase of membership sales more in chambers of commerce than our language. Every word spoken carries inspiration, persuasion, and hopefully, commitment from businesses to act. Salespeople can tap into the power of their sales presentation by deconstructing and embedding language fundamentally reflective of the human need for safety, security, belonging, self-esteem, and purpose.

My *Chamber World* and your *Chamber World* meet fundamental human needs regarding safety, security, belonging, self-esteem, and purpose in almost everything we do. Think of our impact on human needs every time we advocate for business-friendly policies. These policies can ensure or disable economic stability and job *security*, impacting the livelihoods of both business owners and their employees, all of whom just happen to be human.

Membership further creates a sense of belonging to a community of small and large businesses with programs and events chambers provide for customer development through networking. Membership can then elevate the esteem of active businesses and their status among the community through recognition and public endorsements.

Human needs are the same needs of every business operated by humans. I found every level of Abraham Maslow's hierarchy of human needs led me to a hierarchy of conversation levels that related our work to their work and our needs to their needs. It deserves our continued research in building membership sales conversations.

Understanding the unique needs and priorities of each corporate prospect and tailoring the sales presentation accordingly can increase the likelihood of closing more prestigious and valuable memberships. By focusing on specific benefits that resonate most with each prospect, salespeople can effectively address objections and secure commitments. By putting the needs and interests of this target market front and center, sales professionals or volunteers can build trust, rapport, and ultimately, secure long-term memberships, which will feel like partnerships to new corporate members.

It's not about charm; it's about connecting the value of the chamber to what they value. Their values, from their vision and mission to their products and services are all listed on their corporate websites. *(Secret)* Go find what their world has in common with our world and customize each presentation. Again, comparing chamber values along with our benefits and features and how they relate to the products and services of a potential member, big or small, will make cold calls warmer and our relationships more relatable.

Chamber salespeople must understand the unique needs, priorities, and expectations of each prospective member by engaging them with questions that bring out the business motivations and challenges they have. This method sets the stage for a custom presentation that speaks to the specific needs and values of the prospective member. Strong sales conversations will keep connecting the dots between the mission of the chamber and the mission of every business prospect.

We can show how our work, combined with their work can amplify and multiply what

TELLING OUR STORY

they're already doing. The strength of a chamber of commerce lies in its total membership. By prioritizing the attraction of large businesses, tailoring sales approaches to individual company needs, and championing the vital role of your chamber for business in your community, the chamber is destined to cultivate a substantial and influential membership base. This foundation enables us to push for progress and expand economic prosperity by using large businesses to create an eager want in all other businesses to join.

We've discussed the importance of our sales presentations, but the most important presentation doesn't come from you or me, it comes from the customer. How we get the potential member or sponsor to come up with their list of wants and needs begins with the right question. *(Secret)* For me, I would find their wants and needs from their history. As I glanced around their office during my initial meeting with a potential member I would ask this one simple question, "What got you started in this business?" You can often plan on a 20-minute dissertation to follow. When we ask about them, which is always their favorite topic, what they tell us is what we must relate and sell to. When they talk, they buy. When we talk, they might buy.

Based on their business story, which has moved a half-hour appointment into an hour, ask them what would make the chamber a priority business membership for them, their team, and their business?

Members and Guests

We want to engage our members, not disengage them. The most successful chambers, associations, groups, and clubs exist because of these two words, "Members Only." Simply stated, it means if you're in you're in, and if you're out, well, you're out.

Allowing certain people to bend the rules of participation undermines organizations that require membership. *(Secret)* Bending the rules bends the organization's foundation. We subliminally lose the respect of the person we are bending the rules for, and we will ultimately lose the people that agree to play by the rules.

Successful organization executives understand that membership comes with exclusive privileges. If someone is a member, they enjoy these benefits; if not, they miss out. While membership has a price, the cost of not being a member is the value of opportunities and advantages they forfeit.

TELLING OUR STORY

That said, there is a desire to be inclusive because we want everyone of course to be a member. So, protect these prospects; let's not call them names. Calling someone a non-member is demeaning and it appears that we are trying to shame them into joining. Recruitment of these members will always be difficult, and "non" is always a negative term. From "non-profit" to "non-member" it always starts a negative conversation.

Avoid the term "prospective member" as well. Prospective member is a fancy way of saying non-member and it still suggests some people are not members which is poor marketing in and of itself. It also suggests that the person is a second-class citizen within the organization. When we introduce someone as a prospective member it always suggests that they may not join, or we may not let them. There is still nothing positive here. Avoid the term. To avoid sounding hypocritical, perspective member is appropriate to use in training, but not in person.

(Secret) As for membership organizations, country clubs still say it best--people that are not members are 'guests.' "Members and their guests" are the classic and best way to invite non-members. If there are people (guests) that do not know a member, then assign an active volunteer to the duty. It's much easier for the

active volunteer to recommend membership after helping a guest to enter a program or event under their name. Being a guest is always positive and there is no shame in being a guest. Let the organization earn their membership without underlying negative phrases.

How to Respond to "I Don't Know"

A common response to a question like "Do you want to buy a membership or sponsor an event?" is, "I don't know." It's not because they're ignorant, it's because they simply haven't thought about it. *(Secret)* When someone responds to any question with "I don't know," open their minds with, *"But if you did know*, what would it be?"

I taught this lesson after learning it from a veteran salesman who shared it with me in an industry sales conference. My wife proved its brilliance when she asked, "Honey, what do you want for dinner tonight?" I casually responded, "I don't know," and she asked the magic question, *"But if you did know?"* My mind (and my mouth) immediately came up with, "Uh, spaghetti?" This little question "But if you did know?" allows people an additional moment to answer without the risk of being right or wrong.

TELLING OUR STORY

Keeping potential members talking leads to far more sales than having them listen to us. Relationship building isn't about being charming or charismatic, it's about relating and connecting our values to what they value. *(Secret)* A great personality is always a bonus, but they're not buying our smile, they're buying what we can do to make their business smile. It's paramount that we address how our products and services relate directly to the promotion and sales of their products and services.

By focusing on attracting large businesses, customizing sales strategies to meet individual needs, and advocating for the essential role of chambers in business and in the community, your *Chamber World* will develop a substantial and influential membership base. This strong foundation will empower it to drive changes that are needed to advance economic prosperity.

Catching New Members with "Fish On! Marketing"

On average during my consulting career, I would make over forty roundtrip flights back and forth across North America and I would meet hundreds of new people every year. While sitting with, and meeting another stranger on each flight, I would finally ask the inevitable question, "What do you do for a living?" and 99 out of 100 business professionals would waste the opportunity with answers like, I'm a doctor, I'm an insurance agent, I'm a teacher, or I am a car salesman. All these people told me what they ARE, not what they DO.

When they told me what they are instead of what they do, I would respond with, that's interesting or that's nice, and then wait for the conversation to naturally turn when they would be compelled to ask me, "What do you do, Pat?" Funny, I would say, if I do my job well, I live up to my business card. There's only one response to that answer, "What does your business card say?" And with that question, I've just been given permission to give them my business card which includes my website. If they go there, they will read all about my business story.

(Secret) Here's what we all need to remember; what we are is our title, what we *do* is the end result of our work. Imagine if the doctor would have responded, "I'm in the 'Live long and prosper world," or if the insurance agent said, "I sell stuff people never want to use." With those answers, everyone must respond with, "What in the world do you mean?" The end-result of a doctor's work is for people to live longer and prosper, isn't it? We all buy insurance hoping we never use it,

don't we? The moment someone responds by asking for more information is 'Fish-On!' marketing and the 'end result' lure has worked.

What is the end-result of our work in the chamber of commerce? Some will say "Networking!" when they should focus on the outcome, or better said, end-result of networking, which is *customer development*. What's more attractive to businesspeople: a networking event or a customer development event?

Others will say the end-result of our work in the *Chamber World* is 'advocacy', but the better answers would come from the end-results of advocacy such as job retention, business protection, less regulations, lower taxes, better transportation, better education, and other infrastructure improvement.

I was never a motivational speaker. I was an *activational* speaker. Sure, I tried to excite and inspire people, but it was all for nothing if I didn't offer words to activate the motivation people were feeling. If you want to find the best 'Fish on!" response to, "What does the chamber do?" it should be your mission statement. For me as a chamber executive, when asked what I do it was easy. "We serve, protect and promote our members." When people would ask how we protect or promote our members, I was subliminally given permission to continue selling the rest of our story. If our mission statement doesn't reflect the end result of our work, it's time for a re-write.

The great marketers I know are great salespeople and the greatest salespeople I know are outstanding marketers. We often hear the term *sales and marketing* when chronologically, shouldn't it be *marketing and sales*? Technically marketing begins the process while the sale ends it, but then each entity builds upon the other. Great marketers work with salespeople to research why people aren't buying and more importantly, why people ARE buying. In the *Chamber World* the marketing director is more often the sales director.

Building new marketing campaigns on why people say yes has been consistently more effective in my *Chamber World* career than trying to overcome people who say no. We all go further with momentum. Sales and Marketing should be one department constantly talking and thinking together since marketing is hoping people will act, and selling is convincing people to act.

TELLING OUR STORY

Leveraging Technology

Chamber accessibility is crucial in today's digital age, where being open and available to members and the community extends far beyond physical office hours. We truly are a 24/7 service organization. A robust presence on social medial platforms and a well-maintained and updated website are essential components of this accessibility.

By actively engaging with members through regular updates, informative posts, and responsive communication on social media, chambers can continue being recognized as the epicenter for business and community information.

The great roadblocks in building a higher technology platform for providing business and community information are expertise, efficiency, and of course money. Some basic IT expertise must become a critical requirement in all future job descriptions among chamber employees, including the chief executive officer in smaller organizations. It takes more than one person to consistently provide a strong web presence featuring user-friendly navigation, up-to-date information, and interactive features such as online event registrations, resource downloads, QR-codes plus all the new features that will outdate the list just offered.

Our technology strategies must not only ensure that members can access the chamber's services and information anytime, anywhere, it must ensure members actually want to utilize chamber technology with their day-to-day information needs.

Many believe that technology is the new façade of the chamber of commerce. Our online presence today is far more important than our curbside appearance. And because we all age, we tend to get stuck in an era where we were productive and comfortable with the technology of that time, and therefore resist change.

Can you believe people don't mind change? It's true. People don't mind change; *they just mind being changed.* Here's a timeline that proves this theory:

Circa 1985: "I don't need a fax machine; I've got the U.S. Mail."

Circa 1995: "I don't need email; I've got a fax machine."

Circa 2005: "I don't need a smart phone; I've got email on my computer."

TELLING OUR STORY

Circa 2015: "I don't need a wrist phone; I've got a smart phone."

And so on...

I like to equate this to upgrading our smartphones. The last thing you and I want to do is go back to 'phone school' to learn how the new phone works, so we convince ourselves that our outdated phone is just fine, and we try hard to stop the clock from moving forward until people start passing us by. Learning new technology is hard, but once we do learn, we're angry at ourselves for waiting so long.

Great leaders who want followers to change, use vision as their tool. They paint a mental picture of the future and what it will look like if we simply accept it. John F. Kennedy gave his vision a timeline when he said, *"We're going to send a man to the moon by the end of this decade and return him safely to the earth."*[1] It was all a fantasy until a leader took us there with a vision that said we could actually do it.

When we want our boards to buy in to new technology, we must paint a visual picture in

---

[1] Kennedy, John F. "Special Message to the Congress on Urgent National Needs." May 25, 1961. JFK Library, jfklibrary.org/archives/other-resources/john-f-kennedy-speeches-messages/special-message-to-the-congress-on-urgent-national-needs_05251961. Accessed July 29, 2024.

their minds of what the change will look like. People don't mind change; they just mind going to phone school.

Paint a Picture with New Technology

A successful website hinges on three keys: Traffic, Traffic, and more Traffic. If we can't answer why someone should visit our site more than once, we need to rethink its purpose. Our website should be a tool that members, sponsors, and the community rely on regularly. Every business office, especially anyone who serves as a company's information specialist, should have the chamber website as their daily go-to site and if it doesn't drive their constant repeat traffic, it needs to be rebuilt.

Here's the great question, how long has it been since you utilized your chamber's website? If it's been more than a week for you, imagine how long it's been since your members have utilized it.

Our online presence, including social media, should be profound and worth reading. Avoid over posting random thoughts and instead focus on sharing critical business lessons and important ideas. A disciplined approach to social media ensures we maintain a professional and engaging business presence, attracting, and retaining supporters.

We must demand the best technology and use it effectively while never getting comfortable with what works today and ignoring what will work better tomorrow. In 1994, Keith Woods of the Santa Rosa, California Chamber of Commerce often shared his industry wisdom across the country and was never more profound when he told us over three decades ago, "We can't afford to be on the cutting edge of technology, we must consistently be on the *bleeding edge* of technology." *(Secret)* There's nothing worse than an antiquated chamber of commerce. If we don't invest in the latest technology, it will ultimately impact negatively on the entire organization.

Today, if I'm in the *Chamber World* and need consulting on technology, the first name I would call is Frank Kenny. Frank's work has become essential for chambers wanting to stay on the bleeding edge of technology. I don't think Frank will ever be old because he's too busy staying new.

Now Make Some Noise

Once we have the best tools of technology and everything is working well, it's time to make some noise. Noise is defined as a sound that causes a disturbance and disturbance can be a powerful tool in marketing our value. Consider the big screen sports stadiums that demand their fans "MAKE SOME NOISE!" when trying to heighten their team's momentum. The result is a wave of sound that inspires the home team and *disrupts* the opponents.

During my tenure at the Coeur d'Alene, Idaho Chamber of Commerce, we were acclaimed "The Most Successful Chamber of Commerce in the Pacific Northwest!" which included the larger metro Chambers of Boise, Idaho, Portland, Oregon and Seattle, Washington. How did we do it? By making noise.

Once we reached the 1,000-member mark, it was time to do even more promotion instead of resting on our laurels. Whether I was addressing a local audience or a conference of my peers, I would boldly acclaim our successes and numbers. When challenged by the Boise Chamber who then had 1,700 members, I pointed out that our membership numbers were more impressive given the difference in populations. Boise was a community of approximately 230,000 people, nearly ten times the size of Coeur d'Alene

TELLING OUR STORY

which was then 24,000 in population. The math supported my personal acclamation.

This blatant acclamation inspired our members to strive for even greater success. No coasting here. When you have momentum, keep leading and make more noise every chance you get.

On the other hand, we need to know when silence is more powerful than noise. (Secret) When things go wrong and negative media swarms, the instinct might be to respond loudly and defensively. As mentioned earlier, being quiet is counterintuitive but invaluable. Silence allows negative issues to dissipate naturally without further escalation. When faced with a firestorm, take a breath, seek wise counsel, and keep quiet. This too, shall pass. Keeping silent can help mitigate damage and allow the chamber to recover gracefully.

By operating with urgency and visibility, making strategic noise, and knowing when to stay quiet, chambers can navigate challenges and seize opportunities. Leveraging technology and maintaining a strong online presence are crucial for staying relevant and engaging. These strategies ensure that chambers of commerce remain indispensable to their communities, driving growth and a sense of belonging.

CHAMBER WORLD

Rationalizing Social Media

I hold a love/hate relationship with social media. When social media is used well, it is a magnificent tool for expanding connections, information, and relationships. When abused, it becomes a narcissistic and selfish platform expounding misinformation, losing connections, and destroying relationships. Social media magnifies our loves and our hates, often creating an overwhelming environment we must learn to manage and control.

I've often referred to Facebook as grown-up show and tell. It was perfect for people like me who need attention and for keeping my name top-of-mind so my "friends" would think of me when they needed a speaker, facilitator, or consultant. It was terrific subliminal advertising at no cost until I began analyzing the time I spent writing, scrolling, and counting my 'Likes." If time is money, I was going broke. This was especially true when I began counting the other platforms I was on. Not only is my greatest competition in the mirror, so are my greatest problems. It was time for an eye-to-eye meeting again with the mirror.

Chamber World is a huge social world in and of itself, and social media magnifies it. My definition of justify is in the word. *Just if I* look at it this way, or *just if I* look at it that way. When justifying, I'm usually trying to validate something that I know is wrong for me. Being honest with ourselves can be hard because the truth hurts. The good news is that truth only hurts for a moment, while a lie hurts forever.

It's The Little Things

Keeping the negatives quiet and the successes loud can be impacted by the little things as well. There is a common practice throughout our industry that undermines this thinking when we announce when the office will be closed. What? We're open 24/7 online. Technically, we never close. When the physical office is closed have a sign with a QR code stating exactly that; The *MyTown* Chamber of Commerce is Always Open 24/7 online.

It's a marketing rule. Never tell people what you aren't when you can tell them what you are. Using valuable communication channels, especially an additional email interruption to broadcast a holiday office closure, is counterproductive.

The worst sign any business can put on their door is OFFICE CLOSED. That will be the day most of our customers or members happen to drive by. We don't have to state the obvious on weekends or holidays. Instead, the focus should be on when we are open. Using valuable member emails to announce WE'RE CLOSED on holidays is far from the best noise we can make. *(Secret)* Let it go and instead, promote and remind members of our interactive online presence for holiday information.

If we must advertise our office hours, list the days and times we are regularly open. Our members are adults and can figure out when we're closed on their own. Again, keep the negatives quiet and the positives loud.

Chambers of commerce are historically positive organizations, otherwise they wouldn't say, "We're having a chamber of commerce day," when reporting great weather. Embracing a culture of positive, unapologetic value, prioritizing financial health, and maintaining 24/7 accessibility are not just operational strategies – they are the essence of our mission. Together, these principles ensure that chambers remain the heartbeat of vibrant, resilient communities, driving economic growth while creating a sense of pride and belonging for years to come.

Chapter Two

Selling Our Story

CHAMBER WORLD

SELLING OUR STORY

In *Chamber World,* both membership sales and sponsorship sales play pivotal roles in sustaining the organization's activities and expanding a vibrant business community. Each approach, however, serves distinct purposes and targets different aspects of business engagement.

Business memberships are the lifeblood of the chamber. These memberships typically involve recurring fees that contribute to the chamber's annual operating budget. The primary goal here is to offer a suite of benefits that increase the member's business visibility, credibility, and success within the community.

By becoming a member, businesses gain access to a wealth of resources, including advocacy efforts, networking opportunities, educational programs, and exclusive services. The emphasis is on creating a supportive business environment where our members can thrive and benefit from being part of a collective business community.

On the other hand, sponsorship sales are geared towards securing financial support for specific events, programs, or initiatives hosted by the chamber. These sales focus on offering businesses marketing and promotional opportunities in exchange for their investment. Sponsors receive benefits such as logo placement, speaking opportunities, and recognition in event materials which builds their brand visibility and engagement within the community.

Unlike membership fees, sponsorship fees are generally one-time payments linked to events or programs. This approach allows business members to align their sponsorships with their current marketing objectives, gaining targeted exposure and demonstrating their commitment to the community.

Together, membership and sponsorship sales provide a comprehensive framework for engaging with the business community. While membership sales build a strong, ongoing relationship with businesses, creating a network of mutual support and advocacy, sponsorship sales offer strategic marketing opportunities that highlight the sponsor's brand and commitment to community development. By effectively leveraging both approaches, the chamber can ensure robust financial health, drive economic prosperity, and maintain its influential role within the local business ecosystem.

Selling Memberships

Selling chamber of commerce memberships is an art form. If done right, it sells a vision of a connected world, built upon their investments. It is also an instant orientation into the organization. By harnessing the impact of words and crafting compelling narratives that resonate with decision-makers, we can unlock the full potential of chamber membership as a mutual strategic investment for their business and their community. Through emphasizing corporate citizenship, strengthening government advocacy, and framing members as constituents or shareholders, membership can inspire a sense of ownership and commitment among these prospects.

Chamber sales professionals and volunteers who sell for us are urged to maintain a customer-centric approach by addressing objections with empathy and understanding. By doing so, our sales representatives can build trust, rapport, and ultimately secure long-term partnerships.

National sales organizations have taught for years that if you can make the appointment, you have completed 80% of the sale. Think about that. *(Secret)* If they say yes to meet with you, they have said yes to listen to you. If there's interest in meeting, there must be interest in membership. Sell appointments first and fill your calendar with sales presentations that are 80% completed. If we become experts in making appointments, we will become experts in making sales and if we sell to the major players first, we will open the door for making sales to others.

One of the very best appointment strategies is offering optional meeting dates with questions that require 'yes or yes' answers instead of 'yes or no' responses: Would you like to meet this week or next week? (No is not an offered option.) Next week? Great! Early in the week or later? (Again, no isn't an option.) Later? Great! Thursday or Friday? Friday? Awesome! Morning or afternoon? Morning? Great! 9, 10 or 11am? 10? Great! See you then.

They have set the appointment; you just helped. Say thank you and hang up. Statistically, 80% of each sale has been completed. It's easy to ignore or say no to a text or email, so we need to build our conversational skills by asking non-

SELLING OUR STORY

threatening 'yes or yes' questions in making these critical sales appointments.

If a potential sponsor has said "Yes" to a meeting with you, they are interested and more likely to say "Yes" to your presentation. Therefore, great sales trainers focus on selling the appointment before selling the product or service being offered. This paragraph is redundant, but then again, it's redundant. Why? Because repetition is the key to memory, and it's important to remember this strategy.

When making your sales calls, be prepared for roadblocks in scheduling. If they are wavering and not quite there on the "Yes" to meet with you, try offering a prepared ten-minute presentation on the spot. Know your presentation backwards and forward so you're done in under ten minutes and keep in mind that you don't have to explain everything, just list the benefits, and let the client ask questions. This way you keep your ten-minute promise while they extend the meeting asking for more information.

(Secret) Your presentation should include three major benefits of chamber membership: 1) the chamber is their local business information source, 2) the chamber is their business advocacy center and 3) the chamber is their local marketing resource through our

many programs and events. Now, to make it easy, STOP TALKING here.

We don't have to explain any further, just sit and wait for their first question or response. The genius is always in the audience. They know more about their business than we ever will. The moment they respond or ask about any of those three things, we have just been given permission to keep selling. Pardon the term, but when salespeople feel compelled to "show up and throw up" everything the chamber does, we wear the prospective member out. The more they engage with comments and questions, the easier it gets for us. Keep. Them. Talking.

Visualize Success

Before meeting with a potential member, visualize a successful interaction. When you are calling to set the appointment, visualize them saying "Yes" before you call. When you can visualize them agreeing to meet, you will verbalize your part of the conversation at a higher level. Then when you show up at their office later, stop and visualize them agreeing to join just before going in for the sales meeting. Visualizing a positive outcome will create more positive sales than if you didn't take the time to do it. Here's the best part, visualizing that positive outcome takes two to three seconds. That's it and you will be entering every office having already seen a positive outcome.

How does this work?!? Frankly I have no idea. I'm not a psychologist, but once I learned how powerful visualizing a positive outcome was, I never stopped and while I may not know how it works, I have a good idea why it works. It's always easier to go somewhere you've been to before. Going someplace new seems to take forever while going home takes no time at all. Why? Because you've been there before. If I can't see the sale, it's always been harder to make the sale. Always approach your sales calls with an intent to 'see it well, say it well and sell it well'.

If you have been in sales for any amount of time, you have heard this famous response when salespeople are trying to figure out why people don't buy. The answer goes like this...Some do, some don't. Some will, some won't. So what? Next. It's a truthful answer to the wrong question. Successful salespeople ask, "Why *do* people buy?" These salespeople find answers by reviewing only those who say "Yes!" Those who do and those who will create momentum, while those who don't and those who won't destroy sales momentum. Focus your energy on those who create momentum.

Use Expert Power

If knowledge is power, then education and research is empowerment. The most successful salespeople empower themselves by becoming experts first and salesmen second before succeeding in sales. Salespeople who are genuine experts on their product or service impress every potential client they serve. More than that, experts earn the trust of their clients long before those who don't take the time to educate themselves and research their potential members.

If volunteer sales are your strategy, the critical team for any chamber is the Membership Development Project. (I prefer projects over committees and tried to avoid the term ever since learning that a committee is a group of people who take minutes and waste hours.) This project is dedicated to expanding and enriching the chamber's membership base. Their responsibilities include developing membership drives, crafting compelling value propositions, and 'sealing the deal.' The Membership Development Project is all about recruiting new members.

The most successful volunteers take the time to know and understand the organization by studying and memorizing the names of all current Board members, committee chairs, and major sponsors. They memorize historical names of the prior generations of Board members. Why? Because knowing these names suggests that people on those lists know the volunteer's name as well. It's a powerful image and prospective members feel they are listening to someone on the inside.

The key to helping volunteers research and develop an expert approach is to do it for them. Staff need to take charge and develop a portable sales presentation that will support the Membership Development Project. The presentation should include the chamber's vision, the mission, and the strategic plan, with a short explanation of each. Then follow up this training with five-minute agenda items regularly at membership development project meetings to update and build upon their presentations.

The knowledge of these expert volunteers gains the highest respect. They know the chamber and all its programs by rote. They can speak to the benefits of membership by rote. They know who's who on the board and who's who within the membership. An expert volunteer salesperson is impressive. They gain instant trust and give every potential member confidence in joining or sponsoring without any sales tricks or gimmicks. The great benefit for these sales volunteers comes when they make future calls for their own company as they are already known and already trusted.

Beyond knowing who's who and what's what, if we want to talk an even bigger game, we need to make a list of what our chamber has done to lead and support the advancement of our community *since it was chartered*. It's a big job that results in bigger sales. When they ask, "How much does it cost?" we can say, "In essence, every membership is pre-paid." When we do the history, the past successes of our chamber in promoting new schools, new hospitals, new roads all lead to where we are today.

Go back and research how many times local leaders circled the wagons at the chamber of commerce to campaign for new infrastructure helping our communities grow. Nearly every success we've had throughout our local *Chamber World* has gone on and on into perpetuity paying dividends back every year, and leaders keep coming to the chamber with new infrastructure needs to keep building and growing our communities.

All those names and all those successes are like built-in testimonials. Knowing who's who today and who was who yesterday is critical in telling and selling our story. We talk about the importance of the chamber being 'at the table'

SELLING OUR STORY

but look at what happens when leaders come to the chamber's table. Airports, hospitals, schools, and other major developments were often born at the chamber table in most communities nationwide. This is the reason why proactive businesses enter the local *Chamber World*.

With expert knowledge of the chamber, people will already feel like a member even before they say yes. Keep selling with knowledge and research because the more we know, the less "no's" we'll hear. And if you do hear a 'no', follow up! Persistent and consistent salespeople know that follow-up is a critical key to sales success. *(Secret)* Persistent follow-up impresses more than it depresses business owners and managers. Unfortunately, chambers often have a high turnover rate of salespeople because our members hire the best ones away.

Selling memberships is hard because of us, not them. Relax; being too anxious to get the sale is what makes it hard. If we've been granted the appointment, we've been granted the time, so take the time and present the chamber with just enough information to build more curiosity so they'll ask more questions. Less is always more when presenting a product or service. Is it easy? I wish. It takes hard work to make selling easy.

Tier Options to Fit Budgets

Every salesperson wants every potential member to reply with the 'Yes' word more than any other word during a sales presentation. But how? The best lesson I know is to only ask questions that require a "Yes, of course" answer: Do we want a stronger customer base in our community? "Yes, of course." Do local businesses want a supportive local government? "Yes, of course." Do local businesses want low cost, high return marketing programs? "Yes, of course."

(Secret) The greatest transition from presentation to closing is to say, "Let's see what this looks like on paper." In closing memberships, you can offer three tier options on paper to say "Yes", without an option to say no. For example, "Which of these three options fit your needs and your budget the best? The Triple AAA, Double AA, or Single A tier? Again, there's no room for "No" when offering options, but no more than three. Great salespeople offer their products and services with three options and then stop talking.

Write out your own questions that require a "Yes, of course" answer and make them a full part of your sales presentation. The key is to get people used to saying, "Yes, of course"

SELLING OUR STORY

during your presentation as if it's a habit so it will become a natural response when closing. It takes time and practice but well worth it if you love hearing "Yes, of course" as much as I do.

Now let's talk about objections. There are many, but here are the top three objections that never go away:

Objection #1: I don't have the time

'I don't have the time' is a common objection and hopefully, that's our fault. If they don't have the time, it suggests that business is booming, and we've been doing our job building a strong business environment for our members. When they say they don't have the time, let them know that the last thing we want is people with time on their hands. We're an organization of busy people and busy people get things done.

Our response should also include that we don't need their time as much as we need their name and their money to support our work. That's the beauty of it; chamber staff and engaged volunteers do all the work on behalf of members who don't or won't take the time to participate.

It's their money that pays for our work, but it's their *name* that creates the impact of our work to protect and serve their business community. When potential new members express concern about how much time it would take, we can first suggest assigning their membership to a marketing or sales director. Sometimes a company's human resources director is the ideal person to represent a member business. That said, if they still don't want to allocate anyone's time to the chamber, focus on the importance of their name making our constituency that much stronger. *(Secret)* We need their name far more than we need their time.

Objection #2: I don't have the money

Isn't that exactly why we exist? Our work is so they never have to say that again. An excellent argument to overcome the *"I don't have the money"* objection can be made when discussing the difference between the price and the cost of membership, which is significant. *(Secret)* When a member asks, "What does it cost?" the most effective response is, "If you join...or if you don't join?"

Here's where we can show that the price may be $600 to join, but the cost of not joining will be lost opportunities and connections. If a member's sales or marketing director can develop at least three new accounts by working once or twice a month within the chamber's programs and events, the $600 is usually well covered.

The *"I don't have the money"* objection usually isn't true. What they mean to say is that the chamber isn't a priority. This is an excellent opportunity to show our value. We can usually compare one annual membership to one week of an entry level employee. If a company has the money to hire a part-time, thirty-hour entry level employee for a starting wage of $15 per hour, we know they have at least $450 in the bank to spend.

Now we can suggest they consider employing the chamber's five full-time employees to work on their behalf for $450 *a year*. We're in business for business and this is a great perspective to share. If they have the money to hire a part-time employee, they have the money to employ the chamber to keep improving their business environment. You might even suggest they think of it as their lowest human resources expense of the year.

Objection #3: The Chamber Doesn't Do Anything for Me

"The chamber doesn't do anything for me," is one of the best compliments we can receive. This tells us that they haven't had to call, and everything is going great! It's also an excellent time to remind them that being a member of the chamber of commerce is like buying insurance. We all buy insurance, but we all buy it hoping we never have to use it. I've told people for years, "I hope you never need the chamber. That tells us we're doing our job well, everything is good, and you haven't had to call with any problems."

This is when they'll challenge me and respond with a current problem, "What about the bad traffic conditions on my street?!" which opens the door to say, "You've got to call us when you need our help, just like we have to call our insurance agent when we have an accident." An insurance agent will never know until we call. The same is true for us, so think of every chamber employee as a member agent, and someone you can call for help.

The smarty pants insurance analogy is an effective response putting our value in perspective, but then the conversation usually continues. When encountering the 'you don't do anything for me' objection, it's crucial to personalize the conversation and highlight specific benefits that align with the prospective member's needs. Acknowledge their concern and ask probing questions to understand their business challenges and goals. Then, tailor your response to demonstrate how the chamber's resources, such as targeted advocacy efforts, educational programs, networking, and marketing opportunities, can directly address those needs.

Be prepared with success stories from similar businesses that have benefited from chamber membership. Close the discussion by emphasizing the chamber's role in creating a supportive business environment that promotes growth and prosperity, ensuring that their involvement can lead to tangible, valuable outcomes for their business.

If You Can't Guarantee It, Don't Sell It

A smart and compelling strategy to get a 'Yes' is to state that there is no risk in joining the chamber. In my *Chamber World*, every membership was 100% money back guaranteed. There's truly nothing like a guarantee to close a membership agreement and retain that member, while there is nothing worse than an unhappy or reluctant member, so give them an out. Tell them if they join and attend three meetings, programs or events within three months and feel it is not worth it, give them their money back.

In fact, you can't give them their money back fast enough. *(Secret)* Anyone who would ask for money back from a civic organization trying to improve conditions within their sphere is the last person we want in the organization. A membership guarantee protects the organization even more than it protects the member because a disgruntled member costs the organization far more than they would ever pay in dues.

Without question, the easiest purchasing decisions happen when a buyer feels no risk. When chambers offer a membership guarantee, it takes all the risk away. Guarantees also prove our commitment and confidence in the value of our memberships. Yes, people have dropped after their first year, but the only people who would ask for their money back after attending and auditing three of our programs or events are the people that would cost us more time, more effort, and more money than their single membership was ever worth.

The *secret* continues by not allowing these people to take up any more time. Rip the bandage off fast so it only stings for a moment. If they audit three different programs or events, and feel their money was not well spent, offer a full refund, and give it with no questions asked. Say thank you, goodbye, and good luck. Stop talking here as well.

SELLING OUR STORY

Put Rejection in Perspective

If rejection is a big issue for you, *(Secret)* get a large aerial view of your marketplace and post it on your sales office wall. Next, start calling the rooftops of businesses to make membership sales appointments and never give up or get frustrated until you have called every rooftop that represents a business in your community.

The good news here is that you will never run out of rooftops to call because so many of those rooftops change businesses underneath. Put a green pin on the rooftops who agree to meet and a red pin on those who reject having an appointment with you. With this strategy, there will always be someone else to call. You'll also like that an updated aerial view with those red and green pins provides a great monthly sales report. Take a picture every month to update your Board.

I used this 'Bird's Eye View' strategy as a national consultant for over twenty years and built a highly successful business using an aerial view of the United States and Canada. For example, when chambers and associations in Texas would stop saying yes, I'd go to the map and call Florida until they stopped. Then it would be Oregon or Wisconsin. It didn't matter. I had 50 states

CHAMBER WORLD

and 10 provinces to call so I just kept calling and ultimately got back to Texas and Florida just when they were starting to say "yes" again. I never ran out of business.

The same can be true in any community. Start calling rooftops in the northeast part of town until they stop saying yes to meet with you. Then start calling the southwest part of town. On average, 25% of a local business population joins the local chamber of commerce so the math says 25% of the calls from those rooftops will say yes. Don't worry and don't focus on those who say "No," just keep calling the next rooftop. A successful salesperson's favorite four-letter word is, next.

Overcoming objections and rejection can be challenging. The reasons and excuses have been heard since time immemorial. Our ability to overcome objections and rejection are found in countless sales books, podcasts, and weekly morning coffee groups of salespeople mentoring each other, so keep learning to keep earning.

Selling Sponsorships

Sponsorship sales are a vital component of the chamber of commerce's strategy to support its initiative in building a thriving business community. By securing financial contributions from businesses and organizations, the chamber can fund a wide range of events, programs, and projects that generate additional economy that benefit the entire community.

These sales can provide businesses with valuable marketing and promotional opportunities, increasing their brand visibility and demonstrating their commitment to local development. Through tailored sponsorship packages, businesses can align their contributions with their marketing objectives, gaining consistent exposure and recognition. This mutually beneficial relationship not only supports the chamber's activities but also amplifies the sponsors' presence and impact within the community.

Everything can be for sale, from advertising on our walls to title sponsorships of annual banquets, golf tournaments, and even parades.

Maximizing Sponsorship Sales

Watching sports on TV, I am continually impressed by the investments businesses make in sponsorships. Businesses value naming rights highly, so we can think of every major event, program, or project we produce in *Chamber World* as a 'stadium' to capture their interest. For example, Business After Hours can be transformed into "The Chamber Business After Hours! Sponsored by the ABC Company" and still be held monthly at different member locations. Electric or gas utilities are ideal sponsors here with a one, three, or five-year naming rights contract commitment.

Let's take a moment for what I believe is the greatest *secret* in selling sponsorships: shut your door, and repeat the following statement as loud as you can three times:

Businesspeople With Spendable Income!

Businesspeople With Spendable Income!

Businesspeople With Spendable Income!

That's right, say it three times out loud. Why? Because this is the target market we offer to every sponsor with every program and every event we produce. The first people we market to are our members. Since membership is voluntary, the very act of becoming a member indicates that our program and event audiences will consist of businesses and individuals *with spendable and disposable income*. They. Have. Money. Not a bad target market for sponsors throughout the *Chamber World*.

SELLING OUR STORY

Every program and event we offer to sponsors also requires participants to spend additional money to attend. Our chamber sponsors become heroes in keeping admission prices lower and this goodwill only adds to the benefit of sponsoring programs and events in the *Chamber World*. This multiplies our value by having this target market of essentially pre-qualified buyers.

We must remind sponsors and potential sponsors that our target market includes businesspeople who are in the business of making more money to reinvest in their own success. If these aren't the people potential sponsors want to attract, it's hard to imagine who would be a better fit for their marketing strategies.

Let's consider the annual golf tournament as an example. Passing up the opportunity to sponsor and interact with people who happily spend up to, and over $500 dollars for a driver (which is a stick with a mallet on the end and only one of fourteen other clubs they have to buy for a set) demonstrates a missed chance to engage with an audience ready, willing, *and obviously able to buy*. Say it again three times.

Businesspeople With Spendable Income!

Businesspeople With Spendable Income!

Businesspeople With Spendable Income!

Keep repeating this mantra in your sponsorship presentations to emphasize how every program and event we offer delivers these highly qualified target audiences.

Relationship Sales Strategies

Effective sponsorship sales are about building relationships and connecting our value to the sponsor's needs. This involves understanding the business and the person we are approaching, demonstrating how our sponsorship opportunities can improve their sales, their traffic, and their brand image.

(Secret) Relationship selling is not about making friends; it's about *relating* our work to their work. Presenting the numbers and showing how our sponsorships directly benefit their business creates a more meaningful and successful relationship.

You may have heard this before, but securing an appointment is also the first step toward a successful sponsorship sale. Offering potential sponsors options that require 'Yes or Yes' responses, such as "Would you like to meet this week or next week?" leaves no room for a "No." Again, this approach increases the likelihood of arranging a meeting.

SELLING OUR STORY

What's Not for Sale?

Continually brainstorm with team members and ask them to come up with any chamber program, project, event, communication, building, equipment, or transportation item that can't be sponsored, and just wait for the "Why Not!?" discussion. If we believe everything can be sponsored, we could uncover thousands of sponsorship dollars left on the table each month. It's hard work initially, but with long-term sponsorship agreements, we can create residual income with little or no additional effort.

Here are concepts and ideas that come to mind that might give you a positive mindset toward sponsoring anything:

- The truck stops and gas stations that sell advertising space in their bathrooms.
- The chamber who had a corporate sponsor pay the lease on their copy machine in exchange for a small, watermarked logo on their letterhead and copies.
- Large corporate members who love purchasing boardroom furniture and tables for the naming rights of the board or conference rooms.
- The chamber shrink-wrapping the program director's car with NASCAR style

advertising to cover the lease and promote a "Racing for Business" theme.

A comprehensive approach to sponsorship sales can significantly support the chamber's ability to supplement membership and support its initiatives toward building a vibrant business community. By securing financial contributions from businesses and offering valuable marketing opportunities, we create a mutually beneficial relationship that amplifies the sponsors' presence and impact while supporting the chamber's mission of serving, protecting, and promoting local business.

Keeping Great Sponsors Sponsoring

Throughout my career, I've had several excellent sponsors who were eager to support our key events. However, I started hesitating to approach them, fearing I was asking for too much, too often. I decided to share my concerns with them, explaining my fear of overburdening them, but at the same time risking them missing opportunities to support new, exciting programs.

Their reaction to my story about a nightmare where a valued sponsor withdrew their funding because they were upset about not being offered a prime sponsorship opportunity made me reconsider my approach. This prompted me to implement a "First Right of Acceptance" policy for premier sponsors. Now, they have the equal chance to sponsor any new program or event before we approach others. This strategy alleviated concerns on both sides, and more importantly, it kept them from running out the back door every time I came walking in the front door.

Managing sponsorship renewals year after year can be time-consuming and costly. To address this, consider creating five-year, no-risk, inflation-free sponsorship agreements. These agreements guarantee no fee increases over the contract's duration, saving sponsors and chamber staff significant amounts of time and money. Additionally, long-term commitments allow for automatic renewals for easy billing unless the sponsor decides to cancel. If sponsors do lose interest and cancel, it often indicates the program or event needs reevaluation. Honest feedback in the form of cancellations can be a valuable barometer for future success.

(Secret) Guaranteeing attendance for sponsorship events can significantly boost sponsorship sales and long-term commitments when they see no risk if it's not well attended. For instance, if we seek a $500 sponsor for a program or event, we should

guarantee a minimum of 50 attendees which works out to $10 per person that we ensure will attend.

If fewer than 50 people show up, offer a rebate of $10 per person under the minimum number of attendees promised. However, if more than 50 people attend, be sure to remind your sponsor(s) there's no additional charge, as those attendees are included in this successful event.

For established programs with higher attendance numbers, offer tiered sponsorship rates with guaranteed rebates based on expected attendance. This approach provides sponsors with a secure marketing investment and encourages us to ensure successful events. On a special note, since I began offering these rebates, I never had one sponsor ask to implement the guarantee. I'm sure it will happen, but it never happened to me.

Chapter Three

Engaging Volunteers

CHAMBER WORLD

ENGAGING VOLUNTEERS

At the core of every successful chamber of commerce is a passion driven by the collective energy and commitment of its members, volunteers, and staff. When that fire is ignited, the room comes alive with animated discussions, hands raised in enthusiastic support, and voices echoing with purpose. This is the dynamic pulse of active participation, another driver behind chamber success.

Engaging members to become a force in your *Chamber World* requires a bit of magic. An inspiring leader, a joint vision and mission that a majority of members can get behind, and deadlines that can put the pressure on to act, not stand by and watch.

Vision is **to be**. *Mission is* **to do**. If you can see it, you can be it. If you can't see it, there's nothing to be. As organization leaders in the *Chamber World,* board members often feel it is their responsibility to establish the vision of the organization when in reality, that should be the role of the president and chief executive officer.

Business corporations, especially local health care organizations, don't hire a person to be chief executive officer, they hire the right person's vision of the organization. When they meet and hire the right person with the best vision and a dynamic passion to lead that vision, board members begin to engage and when they engage, the membership follows with a momentum that is remarkable.

I've often said that vision belongs to the leader and the mission belongs to the missionaries. Once the leader's vision is ratified by the board, both the leader and the leadership, including committee chairs and key sponsors, come together to create a mission statement underlined with a strategic plan or program of work to make the agreed upon vision a reality.

To reiterate, a vision states what we want *to be*, and the mission will state what we are willing *to do* to become what we collectively see in the leader's vision. Look closely at how a great vision with a passionate leader first engages the leadership while the marbles then roll downhill inspiring the committee chairs, the volunteers and ultimately the members watching from afar.

ENGAGING VOLUNTEERS

The Essence of Belonging

Engagement by those uninvolved members watching from afar doesn't necessarily mean volunteering or even attending functions. The greatest barometer of engagement a member makes is the annual payment to renew their membership. The 80/20 rule remains dominant in the *Chamber World*. Twenty percent of the members do eighty percent of the work, while it can be said that twenty percent of the members pay eighty percent of the bills. It's O.K., don't spend time dissecting this split because both sides of the 80/20 divide are engaged and support the other.

Ultimately, chambers of commerce play a vital role in nurturing a sense of belonging within their world by leveraging its membership with a strategic plan or program of work implementing inclusive policies and initiatives and recognizing the financial and physical contributions of their members. Through these efforts, chambers can create a supportive and inclusive environment where all members feel valued, connected, and engaged within the business community.

The greatest tagline I have encountered in over four decades in the *Chamber World* did not come from a chamber of commerce, but a national association of soybean growers. They figured out that the essence of belonging is believing in the work the association does. It was so simple, yet so profound. "If you believe, belong."

If you believe in our vision, belong. If you believe in our mission, belong. If you believe in our work, belong. The first engagement is belonging to the organization that is striving to improve conditions within your sphere. The difference between the *Chamber World* and an industry association is focus. Where industry associations must be all things to one industry, local chambers of commerce must focus on one issue at a time that impacts all or most industries within its boundaries. For us, it's not so much "What's best for your business" as it is, "What's best for your business environment."

Businesspeople want to belong to successful organizations. Success is the great magnet in recruiting, engaging, and retaining members. Leveraging that sense of success strengthens member connections and that in turn strengthens the chamber.

There are many ways that a chamber can create that sense of belonging. Successfully working on advocacy and issues of impact, vibrant community events, educational business support programs, volunteer opportunities, community engagement platforms, dynamic ribbon cuttings, social recognition, and celebration events all reinforce a sense of belonging with the shared pride these successes create. And silly as it may sound, the façade of those dynamics and successes is exhibited in every member business who displays their chamber membership plaque with pride.

The Plaque Attack

Yes. The chamber membership plaque, which is so often an afterthought when it should be a forethought when building a sense of belonging. Great membership plaques reflect the dynamics, the vision, and the mission of each chamber. They are made and designed with quality products to match the quality of our work. A cheap plaque suggests an organization working *on the cheap* while a well-designed, high-quality plaque reflects the value we want members to perceive.

Every now and then we must revisit the relevance and power of our membership plaques. In this age of high technology, you may wonder if there remains value in this standard bearer of membership. Just as university degrees and industry certifications still hold prominence on your wall, so do membership plaques.

For membership salespeople, nothing demonstrates our organization's long-standing stability and credibility better than arriving with a high-quality plaque and setting it on the table before presenting our benefits and features. This is an assumptive sales technique and one that can create a desire and eager want to belong. The substance of that plaque works to physically reflect the substance of the organization all while assuming membership is the right decision.

A well-designed, quality plaque engraved with a member's year of joining, is the first tangible thing we put in their hands so it must reflect our value at that moment and hold that value whenever they glance at it hanging in their office or lobby. I'm a proponent of membership plaques made with wood because on the back of every plaque, it's critical to feature a disclaimer stating, *this plaque is the property of the MyTown Chamber of Commerce and loaned for display to a member in good standing.*

This simple exhibit reflects a commitment to the chamber the moment the business owner holds it in their hands while having their picture taken for the public announcement, and then as we help them hang it prominently in their business. Plaques clearly identify those that are a member. It's an old school membership tool that continues to create ownership for members if the quality reflects the value our chamber wants to display.

Equally important, these higher quality membership plaques are ideal for membership retention. If for any reason, a member does not renew, develop a team of two or three member volunteers whose sole job it is to go into a former member's business to 'recycle' the membership plaque as part of our 'Green Initiative' because after all, it is made of wood. *(Secret)* This team must never use the term that we're *'taking it back.'* We're simply here to recycle their plaque as it is the property of the *MyTown* Chamber of Commerce which most forget and, therefore the reason why we have that disclaimer on the back.

This is something I learned early in my chamber career, and I learned it by accident. A well-known, high profile board member was doing business with a former member who continued to display our plaque. She was beside herself with anger and I suggested she return to the business, not with anger, but with a smile using the recycling language to retrieve it while saying thank you for their past support. She loved it and the delinquent member rejoined before she left.

CHAMBER WORLD

When another prominent board member heard her story, they became a two-person team I privately nicknamed, the Chamber Plaque Commandos. They were fearless and assertive all without being offensive. *(Secret)* Often, a dropped member would rejoin on the spot when those two would walk in to recycle the plaque. "If you have changed your mind, we have a prorated invoice right here to 'reactivate' your membership." This prorated approach would update their membership back to the 90 or 120 days that had gone unpaid.

One more thing before I help you pay for these new, dynamic, ecological, and high-quality plaques. Every membership plaque must state the "Member Since" date prominently on the face of the plaque. Why? Because if a member does decide to drop for a year or two, we will remind them that in fairness to all our other members recognized for their longevity, the next plaque will say, Member Since the date they renew. It doesn't work to keep a member every time, but if it only works once, this book has just paid for itself.

A best practice to fund these dynamic and expensive plaques is to partner with a major utility to sponsor the chamber membership plaque program. This partnership with a utility who can easily afford the expense elevates a chamber's credibility while supporting the utility's marketing efforts to reach more business clients. Utilities have very few competitors so this arrangement allows the utility to cover the cost of the plaques, featuring their logo without causing concern among business members that could otherwise have a direct competitor's name on their plaque.

Little things can make a big difference, Membership plaques, if done well, become another façade of the chamber while silently working as proof of membership, a symbol of engagement, and belonging.

The Inaugural Ribbon Cutting

One of the other well-known and traditional chamber activities where there are plenty of guests that may be future members, is the ribbon-cutting ceremony. This symbolic event serves to celebrate a grand opening or significant milestone, like a grand re-opening of a business within the community.

The chamber's primary purpose of a ribbon-cutting is to provide an energetic and memorable welcome to a new member who is opening a new business. The new members' primary purpose for joining is publicity for the grand opening of their new business. It offers an opportunity for the business owner to introduce themselves and their venture to the community, local leaders, fellow chamber members, and potential customers. Beyond the ceremonial aspect, ribbon cuttings serve as networking opportunities with new businesses every month, allowing attendees to establish connections, build relationships, and support the growth of the business community.

The thing with ribbon cuttings is that we do them so often and so well, people think it is all we do. The number one attraction of joining for a new business is they want a ribbon cutting that we host. The publicity that comes from a ribbon cutting is worth the price of admission and it can blind them to the plethora of benefits and features we offer long after this dynamic inaugural event.

Don't waste a ribbon cutting. Add every member's marketing or sales director to a separate invitation list for every ribbon cutting. There's no better "Leads Group" in town. A ribbon-cutting event can generate publicity for the business on the chamber social media platforms while garnering attention from local media outlets multiplying the visibility we create.

ENGAGING VOLUNTEERS

(Secret) Because of this value, never allow this production to happen without full membership payment prior to the event. If we don't think someone will change their mind about joining afterwards, we just haven't been in the business long enough.

Chambers can make ribbon-cutting ceremonies even bigger by inviting important figures to speak at the event. This not only adds prestige but also encourages regular volunteers to attend, knowing that someone like an elected official or the chamber chairman of the board will be present to personally welcome another new business. A larger crowd benefits everyone involved, enhancing the event's impact. Strategies like these significantly magnify the impact of a ceremonial opening. Consistently elevating the status of these events ensures these openings remain grand and desirable for all who attend.

On the downside, we do these events so much, they can become invisible to those that have been in the chamber a long time. If you are a growing community, you are doing these all the time so it's important to balance attendance and avoid burnout. One way to do this is to schedule a rotation of volunteers so that all the ribbon cuttings are covered. Another way is to rotate which elected officials are invited so the burden isn't only on the mayor or a county commissioner. What's important is to build a relationship with elected officials to ensure they *appreciate the political currency* of showing up for these events. Always follow up with a genuine personal thank-you and public acknowledgement to those officials that do attend.

Aim Them in the Right Direction

The membership drive was fun. The ribbon cutting was amazing. But now, the real reason they have joined comes up in the orientation. This critical in-depth training is essential to membership engagement and of course, retention. In short, we're talking about re-selling them on what they've already purchased. Why? Because they've already forgotten why they joined in most cases. Life is a blur for new businesses, and we need to make our value clear.

Give every member an opportunity to attend this short, but in-depth training while being sure you locate the orientation in a professional training environment by partnering with a corporate member, college or university boardroom that will dictate a sense of importance to the new members and the volunteers participating in the program.

ENGAGING VOLUNTEERS

A strong orientation will teach members how to utilize their membership, and how to get the most from their investment.

If Knowledge is Power, then Orientation is Empowerment

Orientation is critical education for chamber of commerce members for several reasons. First and foremost, it provides new members with a comprehensive understanding of the benefits and services offered by the chamber, helping them maximize the value of their membership. During orientation, members learn about the various resources and support services available, such as marketing assistance, advocacy, and educational programs, all of which can aid in their business growth.

Additionally, orientation offers a platform for new members to meet and connect with existing members, creating networking opportunities that can lead to potential business partnerships and future collaborations. Every chamber of commerce program or event is a customer development opportunity. Be sure their first meeting proves it. Orientation also educates members on how they can actively participate in chamber programs, committees, and events. This active involvement often leads to greater visibility and influence within the business community, enhancing their professional presence.

Now stop.

Before I go on with this tirade about orientation and the importance of where you meet and how you meet, remember who you want to meet. *(Secret)* We not only want to meet the person who signed the check, we want their support team to attend the orientation as well. The hospital marketing director is far more active in the chamber than the chief executive officer will ever be. Human resources directors and other department heads of any business welcome the perk of representing their companies not to mention the benefits to their jobs and careers, so put them on the invitation list.

Now let's continue...

Orientation helps new members integrate into the local business community, making them feel welcome and valued. It provides insight into the chamber's role in supporting and promoting local businesses, ensuring that members are aligned with the chamber's vision, mission, and goals. This alignment ignites a sense of shared purpose and commitment among members.

ENGAGING VOLUNTEERS

(Secret) If you have an easy-to-follow organization flow chart that shows how decisions are made in the chamber, use it! If a picture says a thousand words, and the flow chart usually does, show them at every orientation.

You can use the flow chart, for example, to show how a single member's idea can be sent to a committee and if accepted by the committee, it is then reviewed and forwarded by staff to the president, and from there to the executive committee and ultimately the idea makes it to the board of directors for final ratification, or not. The 'or not' proves that every idea doesn't always make the plan and this 'picture' impresses those who see it for the first time. The organization flow chart is a critical tool to help members *see* how we work in the *Chamber World*.

My favorite and most effective question during an orientation presentation for new members or a new board member orientation is, *"Can anyone paraphrase what I just said?"* Two or three people will speak up and you will quickly learn if everyone is on the same page, or not.

By understanding how to effectively utilize their membership, new members can see a return on their investment through increased business opportunities, cost savings, and enhanced professional development. Orientation also helps establish strong relationships between new members and chamber leadership, staff, and other members, creating a supportive network for business success.

I'm obviously big on orientation being essential for equipping new chamber members with the knowledge, connections, and resources needed to fully *leverage their membership* and contribute to the business community. Dynamic orientations ensure that members are well-informed, engaged, and positioned to thrive within the chamber and the broader business environment.

To make orientation successful, it's a good rule to give members and sponsors a 'carrot' for attending. For some orientations it may be a prize, or a special sponsor discount, and others may have a rule that voting privileges are enacted only after orientation is attended. If orientation is so important to us, then we must make it equally important to them.

Orientation is a Sponsorship Gold Mine

Businesspeople who have just joined the chamber of commerce have proven they are a target market wanting and needing to spend money to get their new business off the ground or wanting and needing to spend money to take their existing business to the next level.

Successful chambers of commerce hold new member orientations every quarter or at a minimum of twice a year. Think how office or building supply companies are always looking for this target audience not to mention insurance agencies, financial institutions or private employment agencies who support new and growing businesses. The list goes on and these sponsors can ultimately become an inclusive first-hand testimonial on the orientation event agenda.

Again, new member orientations are a working example of a customer development program if we remember to make it one. Orientation is win-win-win. We cannot emphasize the importance of orientation enough. It is a celebration of membership into any organization that wants to confirm the value promised to those who have joined. This is truly the first impression every member will have (and keep) of our organization. It can be a great memory, a so-so memory or a bad memory so give it the highest priority.

Every orientation, like every other ongoing program or event, must be produced with the highest possible attention to detail with updated information, a quality setting with tested production equipment that won't fail. *(Secret)* Have a team of leaders *rehearse* and *choreograph* their individual presentations, proving that in our *Chamber World*, we take the new members' investment seriously.

The facts, the figures, and even the fun we can produce at this one event will last a lifetime in the memory of a new member and it just may be the greatest retention program we'll ever have. New member orientation is transformative when it becomes your cornerstone and foundation for total membership engagement.

Control the Narrative and the Media

The first and worst narrative we continue to address in each of our *Chamber Worlds* is the belief that we are a government agency or a department of local government. In every instance we all roll our eyes and ask, "How can they NOT know we are a non-government organization?" The simple answer is, we don't tell them. We seem to be so proud of being a non-profit organization, we forget to add we are a non-profit, non-government organization. We leave that last part out when we should probably drop the first part and only mention the second part.

When we continually remind ourselves and our communities that we are a non-profit organization, it's as if we're apologizing for ourselves and it makes us sound weak. Our narrative is often apologetic and backwards. Keep in mind that our target audience is full of FOR-PROFIT businesses who want more profit.

(Secret) The best narrative is to say *we are a For Profit, Non-Government Organization* and let the non-profit tax status go. Now we can explain how we are *for the profit* of our members and *for the profit* of our community and our tax status is just that, a tax status.

Again, change the narrative and address it only if they ask, "Aren't you a non-profit?" My favorite answer was always, "Only on April 15th, the rest of the year we are working for the profit of our members and our community."

The media covers crashes, not landings. We will never see a headline that says 95,000 airplanes took off and landed successfully today, but if one goes down, it's on the front page above the fold. So, it's 5:00 a.m. Tuesday morning and the phone wakes me thirty minutes early from a deep sleep. It's Grace, my hard charging board chair using her most assertive voice, "Have you read the paper?!?" No Grace, I haven't. She told me to call back as soon as I read the front-page headline story which was, CHAMBER TO FIGHT KOREA TOWN. Whaaa?

It turned out that our immediate past chairman called a reporter and said he was going to get the Chamber to oppose the renaming of his business district to Korea Town, which was being requested by the predominately Korean businesses in that district. It all happened in a vacuum, and I knew nothing about it. Oh boy, here we go.

Later that morning the past chairman called me with an equally assertive voice demanding we take a stand against the name change. I needed more information on what was really happening, and he hung up just before the reporter called me to ask if we were going to fight the name change. I told her, "According to this morning's paper we are, but in reality, the Chamber has just heard about it with your story."

I then told her it sounded like a naming process issue, and I would research it and share my findings with our Board of Directors. She said thank you and good-bye.

Wednesday morning, Grace called me again at 5:00 a.m. with a much more assertive voice demanding I get the paper right now and call her back after reading the editorial cartoon. The cartoon featured eight or nine Ku Klux Klan figures standing around a burning "Welcome to Korea Town" sign with a bubble above one Klansman saying, "The Chamber of Commerce will now come to order." After expressing my frustration with some strong language and startling my wife, she suggested I quickly seek advice from my morning coffee group of mentors.

The greatest advice I ever received when moving to a new community was to find out where 'THEY' have coffee and show up there every day until I was invited to their table. 'THEY' were the people who were the movers and shakers and considered the staid members of the community. I had followed the advice and earned my way to the table. This particular morning, I came rushing in for advice. The most prominent member of the group knowingly and slowly lowered his copy of the paper and asked, "What are you going to do?" I said, that's why I'm here. I'm not sure what to do. I need help.

(Secret) "Don't do anything," he said. "It's their story, not yours. Don't pour gas on this fire." I was surprised. I wanted to know the best way to respond and got just the opposite. By the time I got back to the office, Grace had called an emergency Board meeting to address

the cartoon. Oh boy, here we go! The Board, as angry as I had been, went around the boardroom table with suggestions of suing the paper, writing a strong response, and even dropping the newspaper's membership until one Board member repeated my coffee mentor's advice; don't do anything.

I fully agreed by sharing the earlier advice but added a caveat they all agreed to. A special board meeting would be held the next day, and we would invite the reporter. I asked the Board members to budget two full hours as the *last* agenda item for superfluous discussion on budgets items, including bathroom and office supplies, before acting on the issue. This provided time to bring the temperature down a bit on this topic.

That last action item was a motion requesting local government to develop a formal process for the naming or re-naming of neighborhoods, business districts or thoroughfares. One board member was assigned to make the motion and another to second the motion. Grace called for discussion, and by our plan, there was none. The motion passed in under thirty seconds and the meeting was casually adjourned.

Their great response was to give the reporter two of the longest hours of her life with discussions about purchasing paper clips for the office and toilet paper for the chamber restroom. My board members had the time of their volunteer lives being as boring as you can imagine. This approach worked like a charm and the next morning, on page nine in the local news section was a two-inch column reporting our motion to the county. We really did nothing more than what I offered the reporter in the beginning, but we did it with a subtle statement and controlled the narrative. The story went away.

Sometimes changing the narrative requires silence, but then again, sometimes you just can't resist. A community member was mad about something and wrote the proverbial Letter to the Editor stating, "All those Chamber of Commerce people think about is business!" In response to her letter, I repeated her quote and wrote back, "Guilty." That one-word response was talked about for a week and later came up at our annual meeting. Sometimes the smallest response has the biggest impact for improving our narrative.

Engaging Active Participation

In the *Chamber World*, engagement can include the act of signing and sending a membership renewal check and therefore it doesn't always mean active participation. I define engagement as showing up and participation as going to work. Hopefully, whatever engages our members will ultimately inspire them to activate their support to work on what needs to be done.

Having an inspiring leader take the reins for an important initiative is a great strategy if you're lucky enough to find one. For our Chamber, we had a goal to increase the income from our annual auction. And Lou was the leader we wanted. Once upon a time, in the exciting world of music and creativity, Lou was a man with a knack for making magic happen. He had the Midas touch. From working alongside legends like Buddy Miles to co-producing the iconic tunes for the famous 'California Dancing Raisin' commercials, Lou's journey was filled with one success after another.

At first, Lou flew under the radar enjoying the social aspects of this group until they said it was his turn to take on the leadership role of the AW$UM auction and it wasn't long before Lou's name became synonymous with excellence in our *Chamber World*.

As a business member and a Commodore, our name for Chamber ambassadors, Lou embraced the camaraderie of the group, relishing in the shared sense of purpose. Yet, it was during one fateful meeting of the Commodores that Lou's true leadership shone through. The Commodores challenged Lou with the task of spearheading the upcoming AW$UM Auction. Lou saw an opportunity to elevate the event to new heights.

Standing before his fellow Commodores, Lou issued a challenge of his own—one that would push the boundaries of what no one thought was possible. "I'll take this so-called $15,000 AW$UM Auction on," he declared, "if all forty Commodores will each commit to bringing in a minimum of $1,000 worth of items to sell, and together, we'll make it a $40,000 auction. Otherwise, I'm out."

In the silence that followed, the weight of Lou's proposition hung heavy in the air. But to his surprise—and delight—the room erupted in unanimous agreement. And so, with determination in their hearts and a fire in their souls, the Commodores set out to exceed Lou's expectations.

After the meeting I took Lou aside and asked if he really thought they would go out and bring in $40,000 in donated items? That's when he left a profound mark on my career. "Pat, I'll tell you exactly what they'll do; 50% of these people will bring in just what they've always brought in, while the other 50% have just been given permission to show off."

AND THEY DID!! True to Lou's prediction, just over 20 Commodores rose to the occasion in spectacular fashion. One Commodore brought 15 subcontractors together to build a stand-alone garage/shop for the highest bidder and it alone raised $18,000. The generosity of the audience and the energy Lou brought to the auction seemed to know no bounds. The AW$UM Auction dazzled and delighted, raising an extraordinary $54,000—an achievement that surpassed our wildest dreams nearly quadrupling our old goal of $15,000.

But Lou's impact didn't end there. In the years that followed, every new AW$UM Auction chair wanted to beat Lou's record and the records that followed. With this new success came new momentum. The AW$UM Auction continued to flourish, growing exponentially to a staggering $208,000. *(Secret)* And while the numbers spoke volumes, it was Lou's unwavering belief in giving people permission to succeed that truly left its mark. For Lou understood something profound—he knew that greatness lay not in individual success, but in the collective spirit of people uniting. For the Chamber's other committees, observing leadership behavior such as Lou's was equally inspiring and educational. Lou's success created a rising tide that lifted all our ships.

Heroes, Warriors, and Patriots

We just read a story of a hero. They are the ones who attract actions by their leadership and vision. Their passion and generosity know no bounds, as they invest not only in their own success but in the prosperity of all. They can create a ripple effect in the chamber and therefore in the community with their dedication and focus and can often seem to achieve the impossible.

Just as heroes play an essential role, without warriors, the foot soldiers of progress marching with purpose and resolve, the vision of the hero would never unfold. These are the individuals who heed the call to action, dedicating their time and effort to champion the cause by stuffing envelopes, folding chairs, and selling tickets. These warriors fulfill the mission to every hero's vision.

There are millions of citizens across the country and around the world that have never fired a shot or fought a battle, but they proudly wave the flag, pay their taxes, vote, and stand up for their country. These people are patriots. We also have patriots in our *Chamber Worlds*.

The silent supporters that are steady, quiet, and steadfast. These members may not always be seen on the frontlines, yet their contributions are the bedrock upon which our chambers stand. We must celebrate our own patriots who dutifully pay their fair share every year and wave our flag by posting our plaques, and posters without physically doing much more. Patriot members, often invisible sponsors, and supporters, make up most of our organization so we must always hold and regard them in high esteem.

There are others that we count on to engage with the chamber's activities and programs, though their involvement may not extend to the level of dedication or commitment seen in heroes, warriors, or patriots. However, they still actively contribute to the organization's goals in one special way, simply by staying a current member.

In the dynamic ecosystem of the chamber of commerce, member engagement fuels innovation, drives progress, community growth, and development. We must remember that our chamber of commerce is the façade of our community and our innovation, our progress and growth reflect each community we serve. Yet, within this diverse array of participation, there exists a spectrum of engagement, from the staunch supporters to the ardent volunteers and the visionary sponsors to those members who hover on the fringes, neither fully committed nor actively engaged. Understanding the nuances of motivating and mobilizing these members is paramount to unlocking the full potential of the chamber and harnessing the collective power of its membership.

In the aftermath of the pandemic, the landscape of member engagement has undergone significant shifts. As organizations grapple with the lingering effects, chambers must recalibrate their strategies to reignite momentum and reassert their value proposition. Embracing the lessons learned, chambers can showcase their resilience and adaptability, positioning themselves as indispensable allies to businesses navigating uncertain waters. By leveraging these insights and emphasizing the pivotal role of chambers in the crisis, we can reaffirm our relevance and galvanize support from both existing and prospective members alike.

Leveraging the wealth of wisdom hidden within the ranks of silent influencers, industry leaders, and members who may be uncertain how to engage the chamber, we must articulate the various responsibilities and expectations with clarity and conviction, ensuring that members understand their optional roles and the importance of those contributions. Empowering members to take ownership of tasks and initiatives, aligning their approach with the chamber's vision and values, and moreover, by framing membership as a strategic investment in the collective well-being of the business community, chambers can appeal to the civic conscience and underscore the tangible benefits of active participation.

We Don't Learn It Until We Live It

I love going to church, but there's one part I seldom get excited about and that's the Church Social. Early on, we sat with a couple who attend these on a regular basis. I briefly shared my reluctance to attend "these things" and then asked why they always seemed to be at them. "We come for the success of others," she said. She was one who also liked to be sociably early. "When you hold a party it's a horrible, sometimes crushing blow, when no one comes," she intimated as I shrank in my cushion-less, folding steel church chair.

Somebody here was practicing what others preach at this little Church Social and it wasn't me. This wonderful woman we only knew in passing taught me that it's not about her and it's not about me. It's about others and their needs, not ours. Business books have

ENGAGING VOLUNTEERS

professed for years that the #1 Rule in Business is, "You get what you give" and I thought I knew it and lived it. Not so much. Our new friend was teaching the Golden Rule I was supposed to have learned during church but finally figured it out by attending the Church Social.

With this little epiphany in mind, I thought about our industry and all the ribbon cuttings most people miss, the Business After Hours with marginal attendance and the annual banquet halls only 3/4 full when we recognize the great citizens of our community. We all have a reason to skip, but when we remember to attend for the benefit and success of others, the odds are better that they will attend when it's our turn. "For the success of others," more than a mission, it should be our mantra for participation.

In the end, it's not about individual achievements—it's about the success of others. Just as attendees at a church social come to increase the success of others, members of a chamber of commerce are supposed to gather and champion the accomplishments of their peers. It's a reminder that true success seldom happens in a vacuum, it lies in lifting each other up together, in supporting a community where every member thrives, thereby elevating ourselves and our community. Another rising tide, eh?

And yes, now when I attend church socials, I go with a purpose and a smile.

Getting Members to Volunteer

"Why don't people volunteer?" The most popular answers include that they don't have the time or, nobody asked them. Two facts can debunk these responses. First, we all have the time, in fact we all have the exact same amount of time every day.

What we don't have are the same priorities and therein lies the hallmark of how the busiest people get the most things done. Great volunteers seem to make helping others their priority and instead of saying yes and putting it on their list of things to do, they use their 'listing time' to just get it done. The great ones are self-aware of their own competence and capabilities, and they thrive on one accomplishment after another. It's not about time when people don't volunteer, it's about priority.

Nobody asked? That's hardly true because we ask all the time, we just don't ask correctly. "WHO WANTS TO STUFF ENVELOPES?" ... Nothing. Crickets. Why? We didn't ask correctly. Now try, "We need three people at noon tomorrow who can stuff, seal, and send 1,200 pre-stamped envelopes with raffle tickets to raise ten thousand dollars." It's not them, it's us.

We seldom offer enough information when asking for volunteers. The more they know, the more they volunteer. Let people know they won't be alone by asking for three people. You'll probably get more but if you don't, the one or two you do get will work like heroes. Define how much needs to be done in a certain time period and compile the work into three steps before closing with the purpose and goal of the project.

People knowing what to do is the first step to increasing volunteerism but not knowing *how* to do what you want done is a roadblock many of us forget to address. On-the-job training is a terrible (and dangerous) strategy for volunteer development. This means taking the time to know what you want and sharing the roles, rules, and regulations in volunteering for anything from ticket sales to parking cars at the big event. Preparing volunteers to serve on committees, projects, events, and especially the board of directors requires serious orientation and training.

Imagine asking for a volunteer to umpire a softball tournament when they haven't studied and learned the rules. We're voluntarily setting ourselves up to fail and with more and more issues of legal liability, it's incumbent upon us to continuously offer effective and efficient volunteer orientation. *(Secret)* When we take the volunteer training seriously, volunteers will take the work seriously.

All member and volunteer engagement or participation requires *continuing* education and training as programs and events evolve. Building a training program for new and renewing volunteers while having it in place and regularly scheduled must be the initial priority in volunteer development to increase long-term participation and engagement.

Allowed To Be Big

Beyond volunteering, the ultimate member participation and engagement strategies naturally include attendance at our programs and events. We want big crowds but fail to recognize the biggest problem in attracting more people is space. We forget that if we have a room that holds 200 people, it limits us to 100 members when we remember to include their spouse or partner who will likely attend. The Plus 1 factor becomes an invisible roadblock to building large member audiences.

How does a chamber of commerce with a community population of 24,000 people reach the goal of 1,000 members like we did in Coeur d'Alene, Idaho? We were lucky. We had a singular business leader and visionary who saw our sleepy little lakeside community as a beautiful lakeside *resort* community. He built the beautiful Coeur d'Alene Resort featuring a 1,000-seat conference center. Those thousand seats finally allowed a small chamber to go big.

I only wish I could highlight my dynamic leadership skills or my great organization management prowess for this success, but truth be known, our phenomenal growth didn't reach its potential until we were allowed to be big. If you don't have a big room, it's difficult to have a big chamber.

Once organizations figure this out, they get creative with barns, warehouses, airport hangars, huge tents on high school football fields or pavilions at county fairgrounds. They move their annual meeting date out of the ice-cold month of January and schedule spring, summer, or fall dates that accommodate the best facility in going for bigger audiences. If it takes a bylaw change to go big, so what? Just

CHAMBER WORLD

do it and don't allow a little work to interfere with a big vision.

If your *Chamber World* isn't allowed to be big, make allowances so you can be.

Chapter Four

Let's Talk Money

CHAMBER WORLD

LET'S TALK MONEY

In every successful chamber of commerce lies a powerful engine—an engine driven by deliberate foresight, thorough financial planning, and the unwavering dedication of its professional and volunteer teams. When this engine runs at full capacity, the organization flourishes—data transforms effortlessly into actionable insights, and every dollar is allocated with precision and purpose. This embodies the essence of operating effectively and planning with prudence, forming a bedrock for chamber success.

Understanding the economic landscape, and making informed financial decisions are not just tasks—they are the responsibility and lifeblood of a vibrant organization. It's about more than just numbers on a spreadsheet; it's about crafting a future where the chamber can continue to serve its membership and community with the finances it manages efficiently and effectively.

CHAMBER WORLD

Monetizing Our Value

The ability of a chamber to attract funds is directly tied to its presence, its brand, and how it is perceived by its members. By embracing a culture of unapologetic value, chambers can confidently and clearly champion their organization's worth. To have an organization like ours open, operating, and ready to respond to issues impacting our members requires serious and consistent funding.

Over the years I have found two conversations about funding the chamber to be the most compelling. The first is to provide the facts and hard data of where the money goes because many members dismiss or forget that chambers have the same *monthly* operating costs they have. Our accounts payable include employees, insurance premiums, rent or mortgage payments, along with utility bills, office equipment and maintenance costs month after month while members only pay once a year. A $400 annual membership equates to less than $35 per month toward funding a chamber's twenty to thirty thousand dollars in monthly operating bills.

For example, helping members understand how far a $400 membership goes in a $400,000 operating budget, puts their dues into a more compelling perspective. Often, showing our 12 months of operating expenses, compared to one annual membership, illustrates its excellent investment.

Small chambers with as low as a $100,000 operating budget usually have 150-200 members. At $400 each, they don't begin to reach the total cost of operations, and they have to make up the remainder through programs and events.

When calling to thank members for their renewal check, I would remind them how far their $400 went by saying with a smile and my tongue in cheek, "With your check, we only have $390,600 to go." *(Secret)* There's really nothing like perspective to show members the importance of each membership.

The second conversation that follows is the what's-in-it-for-me discussion. As much as we want to scream, "*WE'RE NOT IN IT FOR YOU! WE'RE IN IT FOR YOUR BUSINESS ENVIRONMENT*" we must temper our frustration and keep breaking it down for them.

When prospective chamber members ask, "How much does it cost?" as previously mentioned, it's best to respond with a question of our own, "If you join or if you don't join?"

The critical juncture in this conversation is to now stop and wait for the question.

"What do you mean?" With this question, we have been given permission to tell our story. We can feature the customer development programs for company marketing directors to attend, the latest human resources regulations being featured in our monthly business seminars for company human resources directors to attend, and their company name not being included on our 'Power List of Business Constituents" when fighting for or against government taxes or regulations.

It's hard to be apologetic when you can make a $400 annual membership seem like lunch money compared to the expenses that must be paid to operate an organization that provides the business support and protection we do. However, some will still need more convincing.

The Essential Return-On-Investment

The return-on-investment can be explained *and monetized* in a straightforward comparison between the issues we address and individual budgets our members have to meet. Monetizing the value of our work in comparison to the budgets they are pressured

LET'S TALK MONEY

to meet every year can justify our dues if we can help paint a picture for them, like I did for Mr. Anderson below.

"Visualize for a moment Mr. Anderson, four businesses at the hypothetical intersection of First and Main Street in *AnyTown*, USA. Let's propose that our chamber has a minimum impact of one percent (1%) on every business budget surrounding this intersection. This is how our pricing becomes relevant to the gross annual income of each member, no matter their business size."

Then I would start drawing the picture, "Working clockwise on the northeast corner of First and Main is a small retailer that earns an average gross annual income of $100,000. Just south of this small retailer on the southeast corner, is an independent insurance agency grossing $1,000,000 in annual premiums. Across the street to the west is a popular jeweler bringing in $5,000,000 annually and just above them, in the northwest corner of our intersection, is a Big Box store doing $50,000,000 per year."

Now I'm ready to provide a simple, yet powerful example that monetizes our value. "All four businesses in this hypothetical location are suffering from the fact that there is no traffic light or stop sign to manage the traffic and people are avoiding the intersection of First and Main because of the traffic chaos. The independent insurance agent who happens to be a chamber member, calls for help to petition the city to solve this traffic problem. Now, because this is exactly why we exist, the chamber enthusiastically goes to work immediately gathering data and traffic counts to present the argument before the city council. Ultimately in our scenario, the chamber is successful, and the traffic light goes in making it easy for customers to come and go."

This is when I suggested to Mr. Anderson that the value of the new traffic light to each business in this hypothetical location should amount to a minimum increase of 1% for each of the businesses involved. "So, let's do the math," as I finish the picture for him.

"With a minimum 1% impact, and it's obvious the impact will be higher, the small retailer will increase his annual gross sales by $1,000, ($100,000 X .1 = $1,000) so he is now earning $101,000 per year without doing a thing. The insurance agency's one million dollars in gross income goes up one percent, or $10,000 per year while the jeweler increases sales to $5,050,000 per year. Finally, the Big Box annual gross income of $50,000,000 goes up an additional $500,000 with no additional effort or time required."

This is what chambers of commerce do for their members and the business community every year in every town when asked to help, but then, no good deed goes unpunished. The Big Box or the jeweler might say they don't need us any longer so why should they join if their big problem is already solved?

This is where the chamber's one-time effort proves to be our long-term value. That stop light isn't coming down at the end of the year. It will continue to provide a full return on investment for every membership every year supporting even more traffic and more growth. Now it's as if all four of the annual membership investments on that corner have been pre-paid and any additional work on other issues will make their annual membership even more valuable.

More often than not, the success of our work on business issues goes forward into perpetuity. Our value only grows. In the hypothetical case above, the successful work of the chamber will repeat itself with that stop light every day, every month, every year. For these businesses, these additional years of income growth from that stop light's impact will offset any cost of membership, perpetually. We just have to remind them from time to time.

And we don't just work on stop signs; we work on all issues that affect businesses within our areas of influence. I was taught that the 'four' keys to economic development are transportation and education--education and transportation. Yes, those two are duplicated because they are so important! Those topics alone will keep a chamber's issue development agenda full, year to year, along with other topics that come up.

In essence, membership dues employ the continuing work of the chamber. Whether it's advocating for policy changes, providing essential business resources, or producing marketing opportunities, the chamber's efforts ensure a thriving business environment and if just one issue, one time has a positive one percent impact, we have nothing to apologize for when pricing our memberships and services.

By investing in any community through chamber membership, local businesses are insuring and securing the ongoing support and advocacy of their local chamber, every year. And while the chamber isn't always successful with every issue, it only takes one successful event to offset the annual expense of membership into perpetuity.

Thus, the return-on-investment for chamber membership is not only immediate and measurable, but also long-lasting and multifaceted, reinforcing the critical role of the chamber in sustaining a vibrant local business environment.

Avoid the "F-Bombs"

No! Not *that* F-Bomb. The F-Bombs I'm talking about are FREE and FUNDRAISING. With the proof of our return-on-investment above, it may sound like chamber membership is free, and that is not the case. Free may work in promotion for some industries, but not in the *Chamber World*. I've often stated that FREE is an "F-Bomb" in our industry. Simply put if something is free it's worth missing or worth being late for. If it doesn't have a price, it doesn't have value.

Free is an attractive term for promotion in some industries like retailers and airlines, but for chambers always trying to sell and promote our value, it just doesn't work. The word 'free' lessens or cheapens our value every time so try to avoid 'free' at all costs (pun intended).

This all makes sense until those times when the board of directors will say "We are

NOT charging for (this feature or that benefit.)" *(Secret)* If we are not allowed to charge, don't say it's free, say *it's included*.

For example, if we're offering a special seminar on a new business tax law and the board does not want to charge members to attend. Then the best way to market the program while not charging your members would look like this:

NEW BUSINESS TAX LAW SEMINAR
Tuesday, October 8th – 9:00 a.m. - Noon
General Admission: $49
Chamber Members: *Registration is <u>included</u> with your membership.*

The seminar now has a value of $49 to be well worth attending and worth being on time for. Chamber members just had $49 of additional value included in their annual membership. Now, the board is happy, the members are happy, which always makes the staff happy.

FUNDRAISER is the second "F-Bomb" in our *Chamber World*. The moment we use the term *fundraiser* in marketing an event suggests we're broke, which drains our power and kills our image. It suggests that our real motivation is our poor financial situation, and members are secondary to the event's purpose. Lose the term and call the program a program or the event an event, period.

If someone asks, "Where does all the money go?" Tell them, "It's going back to you through M&O, Maintenance and Operations. This Chamber isn't cheap to operate, and we operate for you." In addition, you can add that our programs and events supplement their membership dues keeping them as low as possible.

Fundraisers are ideal for charitable 501(c)3 business organizations because that's what they do. We are a 501(c)6 *business* organization. We are of business, by business and for business. We are not a charity and should never pretend to act like one.

Pricing Like Retailers

Here's a test most staff members and volunteers seldom pass in *Chamber World*. When a potential member asks, "How much is it to join?" An estimated 99.9% of staff and volunteers will jump to the lowest possible price being offered on the chamber rate card. And if not the lowest price because those are only for individual or personal memberships, they will offer the average price that the smallest businesses pay. Please stop doing this.

CHAMBER WORLD

When asked how much it is to join, start with what corporations pay first. "Well, we have corporations that support the Chamber at ten and twenty thousand dollars per year, while smaller businesses invest one to five thousand dollars a year in our pricing system."

We've just told them WHAT THEY DON'T WANT TO HEAR, so immediately follow up and ask what type of business they have and what they were expecting the fees to be. This is when we'll hear them say, "Uh, I thought it would be five or six hundred," when they really thought it would be two to three hundred dollars to join, but now when you tell them there is a $400 level, there is seldom any resistance.

When setting prices for chamber membership, sponsorship, registration, or t-shirts for visitors, always offer them initially at the highest suggested retail price. Oversell them before you undersell them. *(Secret)* The greatest retailers live this lesson successfully every day; *in pricing, you can always come down, but you can never go up.*

Offering a low price in the beginning also says even we don't think our product, or services have much value. This will never be our best marketing strategy so don't fear losing a potential member who wants the cheapest price because the cheapest members are usually the most expensive members to enlist. Have faith in your chamber and in the process of introducing your premium prices first.

Building a Pre-Approved Chamber Budget

Developing, marketing, and selling the chamber budget is a strategic process that requires careful planning, clear communication, and effective execution. A well-constructed budget serves as the financial blueprint for the chamber, outlining the allocation of resources to achieve its goals and sustain its operations.

Building a budget demands a historic review of past performance to justify estimated income and expenses. Marketing the annual budget for board approval involves transparently communicating research findings and expected nuances to leadership during the building process, giving them an idea of what is to come. Selling the annual budget requires us to ensure leadership understands how member investments will be utilized in our mission of driving business and community growth, and how our dollars will clearly support that mission.

Transforming Budgets into Profit Plans

Traditional budgets aim for balance, while a 'Profit Plan' envisions a more positive and ambitious outcome. *(Secret)* Simply rebranding your budget as a profit plan can significantly alter perceptions and expectations. This subtle shift in terminology encourages a mindset focused on surplus and growth rather than just breaking even.

When presenting financial plans, refer to them as profit plans. This approach sets an expectation for having money left over on the bottom line, forming habits of financial prudence and proactive planning. Asking committee chairs and department leaders to adopt this terminology reinforces the idea that every part of the organization should contribute to a financially healthy outcome.

For a chamber of commerce, this distinction is particularly important. Chambers are often seen as providing vital support and advocacy for local businesses. A profit-oriented approach ensures that the chamber not only covers its operational costs but also generates surplus funds to reinvest in business development initiatives, member services and community programs.

When board members review a budget, they tend to scrutinize every line item, focusing on cost control and risk aversion. However, when they review a profit plan, their attention immediately shifts to the bottom line, leading to a more strategic discussion about revenue generation and value creation. *(Secret)* Expenses appear less expensive when viewed in the context of overall profitability, making it easier to justify necessary investments in programs, services, and salaries.

This mindset is crucial for a chamber of commerce, as it allows the organization to maintain a strong financial foundation, enabling it to better serve its members and adapt to changing economic conditions. By adopting an annual profit plan, boards can ensure they are not merely surviving, but thriving and positioning themselves as successful leaders in the business community.

Pay Yourself First

When people ask how I successfully facilitated the rebuilding of three struggling chambers of commerce, I always attribute it to a simple strategy: keeping 10% of our income in the bank. This thinking is of course, easier said than done so I would look at it from a different perspective; while saving 10% of our income might seem difficult, living on 90% of our income is surprisingly manageable.

Look at it from a personal point of view. If you are competent and capable in paying your monthly utility bill, you are equally competent and capable of paying the monthly *Y-O-U*-tility bill as well. Ben Franklin said it best, "Pay yourself first." By consistently *paying* 10% of our income into a reserve fund, we will accumulate a full month worth of reserves every ten months, creating a financial habit that increases that amount over time. In as little as six to eight years, this approach can result in having a full year's income in the bank, ensuring the organization is never held hostage to money again.

Building and maintaining financial reserves is crucial for any chamber of commerce. Reserves act as a financial safety net, allowing for bold, innovative actions without the fear of fiscal instability. A confident chamber becomes a successful chamber and there's nothing like money in the bank to build confidence.

When I took on the challenge of leading three nearly bankrupt chambers, I knew the key to turning them around was building reserves. Without reserves, chambers can appear to be operating hand-to-mouth, struggling just to keep the doors open rather than delivering on the promises made to members. Money in the bank created a positive and confident image.

So, how did we build reserves when funds were so tight? *(Secret)* The answer lies in prioritizing savings, as Franklin suggested. I treated the reserve fund like any other monthly bill. Initially, I adjusted the operating plan to allocate 5% of all income to the reserve fund, gradually but fairly quickly increasing it to 10% as the financial situation stabilized. Living on 90% of our income became a habit and paying into our reserve became an expected expense and psychologically, we treated the money as already paid out and unavailable until we attained the goal of having a year of income in the bank.

Once a chamber has a full year's income in the bank, the focus should shift to maintaining a minimum of six months' operating capital in reserves for those times when you need the reserves. Nothing proved this more than the pandemic in 2020. This minimum balance ensures financial stability while providing flexibility to invest in strategic initiatives or pivoting to emergency programs as they arise. The reserves become a powerful tool, enabling the chamber to undertake projects and initiatives that other organizations might only dream about. For a chamber of commerce, having robust reserves means never having to operate in crisis mode. It provides the confidence to support members effectively, advocate for local businesses, and invest in community development. Reserves transform the chamber's financial conversation from one of mere survival to one of growth and possibility.

To ensure ongoing financial health, make reserves the first "bill" you pay each month. This practice, better yet this habit, fosters a culture of fiscal responsibility and forward-thinking within the organization. Once the habit is established, the chamber can leverage its financial strength to drive community impact and innovation.

They remind us on airplanes every time we fly that we can't help our children or seatmates breathe when we are suffocating. Secure your mask first. This principle applies directly to the financial health of a chamber of commerce. When a chamber member or board member questions the necessity of making a profit on events or raising dues, my response is simple: "How can a bankrupt or poor chamber help anyone?" A chamber with robust financial reserves has far more credibility and capability than one teetering on the brink of insolvency. Which chamber can do more for its members—

the one with $500,000 in reserves or the one that doesn't know if staff will be paid next month? If we're here to support business, we must prove we understand sound financial management in the way we have supported ourselves.

Aligning Expenditures with Inflation

Managing a budget amid rising costs presents a significant challenge in your *Chamber World* and mine. As expenses for services, supplies, and operations increase, chambers must adopt strategic practices to sustain their activities and continue delivering value to their members within an ever-changing economy. This requires a multifaceted approach that includes optimizing resource allocation, implementing cost-saving measures, and exploring new revenue streams.

Understanding when price increases are necessary is vital. For instance, when utility rates go up, so should our prices. *(Secret)* We are not tasked with controlling inflation. Our task is maintaining the viability of our services. If we were worth it before the rates went up, we are still worth it in the next economy. This approach ensures we continue to thrive rather than merely survive. To be successful, we must address inflation and price increases pragmatically and with some perspectives.

For example, in the 1970's minimum or starting wages hovered around $1.50 per hour and gas was .35 to .40 cents a gallon. Jump ahead fifty years and the average starting wage following the pandemic was around $15.00 per hour and gas was $3.50 to $4.00 per gallon. Relatively speaking, nothing has changed in these daily cost arenas; they're both just ten times greater. So why aren't our dues? The point is that the chamber of commerce and its employees are not given any special dispensation on the price of gas, electricity, or housing so we must keep up with inflation to keep and maintain the level of services our members expect from our work.

(Secret) The key to raising prices is to not draw attention to it. Be sure to remember the first two rules in raising prices; The first rule is to do it and the second rule is, don't tell anyone. Do we know any other business that advertise price increases? No. We all know that increases are inevitable, but no one comes out and tells us. We all begrudgingly accept it, pay it, and move on. So will our members.

Yes, one or two out of the entire membership list will call, and when they did it to me, I would immediately compliment them,

"Bob! My compliments! Out of 1,000 members you are the only one to call." Then I would go on about how chamber operations and our employees didn't receive special dispensation on inflationary prices from the utilities, grocery stores or gas stations. *(Secret)* The compliment and simple explanation usually works in retaining members like Bob.

To summarize, when it comes to raising dues and fees, discretion is key. Gas stations and grocery stores never announce price increases, and neither should we. Most members understand the necessity of these adjustments due to inflation. By quietly adjusting dues, we avoid unnecessary backlash. If questioned, explain the reality of rising costs with relatable examples like the increased prices of everyday goods. Most of our members, even when they don't want to get it, do get it, and understand.

Opportunities for Growing Money

Growing financial resources are crucial for the success and sustainability of a chamber of commerce. Some proven strategies to ensure robust financial health and continuous growth include sponsoring or underwriting anything and everything we can.

To reiterate, the message here is to maximize our sponsorship opportunities. Every aspect of your operations in our *Chamber Worlds,* from meeting rooms to office equipment like copiers and phones, have the potential for sponsorship. Every event and every program create an opportunity for a title sponsor. If a business can attach its name to something the chamber produces, it must be available for sale. Successful organizations understand that sponsorships build a sense of ownership among our backers, making them more invested in the chamber's success.

Sponsors as Underwriters

When potential sponsors are hesitant to commit, offer them an underwriting opportunity to guarantee the event or program will take place and in exchange we will offset the fee up to fifty percent.

For example, we need a $5,000 sponsorship to fund an expert speaker's seminar. The seminar is expected to attract a minimum of 100 attendees at a general admission price of $50 per person. By underwriting the seminar, the sponsor guarantees the speaker's fee with a check for $5,000 to the chamber. The chamber is now without any financial risk and promises to repay the underwriting sponsor the initial income from the first forty registrations equaling $2,000. The $5,000 sponsorship is now a net cost of $3,000 and if the chamber chooses to sweeten the deal, it can also include ten registrations for the sponsor's employees or clients to attend. Underwriting can be very appealing when the chamber shares in the program's risk.

Breaking even is a bad strategy

Whenever we catch ourselves saying, "Just so long as we break even," we admit defeat before we start. If a program or project isn't worth charging a fee that ensures profitability, it's time to remove it from the calendar.

The fundamental rule is clear: we weren't hired to break even. *(Secret)* Assign a price to every program and event. The term 'non-profit' refers to our tax status, not our business plan. At that moment when we fear that pricing will deter attendance, it's precisely the moment to set a substantial fee, as it inherently adds value to the program. People have the money; it's how they choose to spend it that matters.

Ensuring profitability for all activities reinforces the chamber's value proposition to its members and stakeholders, demonstrating that it is a vital, sustainable, and forward-thinking organization. This approach not only

CHAMBER WORLD

secures the chamber's future but also builds credibility throughout the community. If you believe image is important, this is the image a chamber of commerce must project.

Chapter Five

Playing By the Rules

CHAMBER WORLD

PLAYING BY THE RULES

Welcome to *Chamber World* governance, where legality, transparency, and proactive leadership guide our organization. Imagine yourself at the helm of a ship navigating through the complex seas of board responsibilities. It's not always smooth sailing – sometimes, it feels like we're charting unknown waters. But with the right tools, the right crew and clear understanding, this journey becomes a story of empowerment and effectiveness.

In the world of organization governance, understanding the legal compass is crucial. It's about guiding your organization towards success while staying compliant, ethical, and transparent.

In the real world of chamber management, the effectiveness of the board is vital. As the driving force behind strategic decision-making and community engagement, a diverse and well-rounded board is essential. It's not just about having experts; it's about curating a team that reflects the community it serves.

But what truly matters is the mindset and behaviors of board members themselves. *(Secret)* The importance of embracing curiosity and vulnerability for a culture of learning and growth in the boardroom and in respecting fellow members' input, as well as their time, is essential.

The nuances of legal governance, proactive recruitment, and finding the balance between challenges and opportunities are situations that every leader finds themselves in at some point. As daunting as the topic of governance may be, the *secret* is delegating it to the right person, chamber member, or legal counselor.

The Legal Compass

Navigating board responsibilities can often feel like venturing into uncharted territory, yet with the right guidance and understanding, it becomes achievable. How can you steer your organization toward success while ensuring compliance and integrity? What steps do you need to take to navigate through all the legal hurdles?

The best legal advice for chambers of commerce is to have an attorney on retainer and/or on your board in an ex-officio (no bias) advisory capacity. Having legal expertise readily available is paramount. Whether through retaining an attorney or having legal professionals on the board, having access to timely and informed legal advice will prove invaluable. Rather than basing decisions on subjective opinions, with a professional legal advisor, chambers can filter all opinions on a clear understanding of the legal implications. This is particularly important on controversial and complicated topics.

Consider the case of a chamber of commerce in a state where recreational marijuana has been legalized. As discussions arise regarding the inclusion of marijuana dispensaries as chamber members, tensions may mount among board members with varying opinions on the matter. *(Secret)* By adhering to the guiding principle of "Legal business. Legal member," the chamber can navigate this delicate issue with a focus on legal compliance rather than personal biases.

By seeking legal counsel, the chamber can gain clarity on the legal ramifications of excluding or including such businesses, thereby assuring a fair and legally sound decision-making process to ensure they don't restrain the trade of a legal business. The last thing a chamber wants is to face a lawsuit.

Knowledge as Power

Don't be afraid to know the law. Attending the U.S. Chamber Institute for Organization Management, the Association of Chamber of Commerce Executives (ACCE) conferences, state chamber meetings, and other continuing education programs provide invaluable opportunities for learning.

These platforms serve as knowledge hubs where chamber executives can deepen their understanding of legal frameworks governing chamber operations. Through workshops, seminars, and networking sessions, attendees gain insights into pertinent laws and regulations, empowering them to navigate complex legal issues with confidence.

By staying abreast of legal updates and compliance requirements, chamber board members can mitigate risks, ensure organization integrity, and make informed decisions that safeguard the interests of their chamber and its stakeholders. Moreover, continuing education programs provide opportunities for collaboration and exchange of best practices among chamber professionals and colleagues, many of whom become lifelong friends. This educational strategy of collaboration offers real-world expertise and effectiveness in addressing current legal challenges facing the *Chamber World*.

Literally, if there ever was a million-dollar reason to attend these continuing education classes and seminars, it's to learn about and know the law. Attending these seminars may scare you to death, as they did me, but go anyway. We can't fix anything if we don't know anything. And then when, not if, you realize how far out of compliance you are, find a young pro bono attorney looking to build a new law practice and put her or him between you and the problem. It doesn't have to be you fixing it; it just has to be you finding the right person who can, and it doesn't have to require a budget line item. Remember, the root word of ignorance is ignore. Don't do it here.

Bylaws: The Backbone of Chamber Governance

It is one thing to know the lay of the land but it's far more important to know the "law of the land." Reading bylaws can often feel like deciphering a cryptic code, and it's no wonder many executives avoid them like the plague. However, embracing this crucial aspect of chamber management can yield significant benefits.

Sitting down with legal counsel to seek guidance on understanding complex sections of your bylaws can not only increase one's comprehension but also elevate one's standing as an astute organization leader. By mastering the intricacies of bylaws, executives and their boards can effectively leverage them as a shield against potential issues coming at us from outside of the boardroom or from issues attacking us from within.

(Secret) Be sure your bylaws give you the structure you need to address challenging situations. Will your bylaws allow you to remove inactive, disinterested or "occupying" board members from the board if they miss three consecutive board meetings? Or if they miss three meetings within a year's time? Put the bylaws between you and the problem. When we can use the bylaws to mitigate our problems, they can be more valuable than our greatest volunteer.

In essence, understanding and adhering to bylaws and seeking legal counsel are essential components of effective chamber management and leadership. By embracing these sometimes impossible to read documents, chamber executives can navigate and lead their organization through another nightmare, upholding organization integrity, and making informed decisions that serve the best interests of our members and communities. To put it simply, knowing, understanding and being able to articulate the bylaws lifts every executive in the eyes of their board members and their peers.

Primary to effective chamber management is the effectiveness of our board of directors. As the guiding force behind strategic decision-making and community engagement, a well-rounded and diverse board is essential.

The Alchemy of Board Composition

The most important diversity in the makeup of your board isn't race, gender, or age as much as it is classification. It is important to align board composition with organization goals and to have the right mix of expertise on every board. Remember, these are the decision-makers that will be directing the organization, so making sure that everyone is rowing in the same direction is essential.

Too many retailers or too many bankers give us an image of being a club or a clique and can also skew the decision-making in a way that is not advantageous to the overall membership community. We must do everything possible to represent the many different classifications from manufacturing to retail, banking to hospitality, and so on.

(Secret) Make it policy to limit the number of board members from one classification so they can truly represent the local business community. We must make every effort to make the board of directors a microcosm of the membership they represent.

Have you ever found yourself on a poorly run board outside of your own organization, where chaos reigns supreme, and decisions lack both rigor and reasoning? In this storm, the absence of a cohesive team is glaringly evident. These problems usually begin with the difficult job of finding and vetting the right people to sit in the right seats of any organization.

Chamber World history has taught me that the standard process of nominating new board members every year is flawed. Starting with nominating up to twelve people for six board openings as a standard process wastes a lot of time and effort. This needs to be changed.

First, the president and chief executive officer or executive director must be fully involved, usually but not always, with the outgoing board chairman. The board chair usually wants to extend her or his legacy offering up colleagues who would take the work forward. The executive wants to be assured the nominated people are competent, capable, and most importantly, *compatible*.

(Secret) Great executives don't want to control the board, but they do want to control the chemistry of the board. We want as much control over the chemistry of the board as possible. The cornerstone of effective board governance lies in crafting a cohesive team, carefully curated to steer the organization towards success. Rather than merely nominating individuals, often known as warm body recruitment, strategic recruitment becomes supreme.

Imagine approaching a potential board member with the words, "Mrs. Williams, we want to recruit you from our member restaurants to lend your expertise to our board of directors." Such an approach not only signals a genuine desire for their service but also sets the tone for a collaborative and appreciative atmosphere. Moreover, pre-approving recruits ensures a seamless integration, shielding the board from the misery of a last minute unvetted disqualification.

We Want You!

If our bylaws say we must 'nominate' ten or twelve candidates for six board positions, get the bylaws changed. If there is no legal reason to require this old, antiquated process, get it changed. We want no 'losers' when it comes to the process of selecting our future directors. Making a volunteer open to being a loser is always a lose-lose proposition for the organization and the nominee. The language and process we use matters.

With well-run boards, recruitment is an art form, a delicate dance of identifying and enticing the right leaders to be at our table. It's about more than just filling positions; it's about sculpting a team with complementary skills and shared vision. Imagine extending an invitation to a potential member with the words, "We have voted to invite you," signaling not just a need for their expertise but a genuine desire for their presence. This sets the tone for a collaborative journey, where each member feels valued in the selection process.

Picture a board where every recruit has been vetted and endorsed, ensuring a smooth transition into their role without the threat of unforeseen obstacles. It's a proactive approach to governance, where the focus is on stability and continuity rather than reactive firefighting.

From the initial recruitment process to addressing attendance and performance, seeking a culture of commitment, accountability, and excellence within the boardroom is a first priority that ensures the board is equipped with the best minds and leadership to navigate the challenges and opportunities that are sure to lie ahead. And to start, let's ask what the greatest characteristic of a board member should be.

(Secret) There are so many positive characteristics wanted in every board member, but none is more important than having the chamber of commerce's board responsibilities be a board member's FIRST CIVIC PRIORITY while they serve.

We've all heard it more than once, "Oh gosh, I can't make it because I have a conflicting meeting" or, "That doesn't work for me, it conflicts with my work on the ABC Foundation." Why can't they tell the other organization that their meeting conflicts with their chamber commitment?

The best chamber board members make the chamber their first priority while they are on the chamber board. What other characteristic matters if they don't show up for us first? Since time immemorial we have said, "80% of a board member's job is showing up."

So how do we find those individuals who will serve the chamber as their first priority? It's imperative to recruit board members whose own personal vision aligns with the organization's vision, and who possess the capacity to contribute meaningfully. An effective strategy involves targeting individuals who hold significant decision-making roles within their companies, such as owners, chief executive officers, or general managers. "These individuals, who issue payments rather than receive them, contribute valuable perspectives and resources." However, it's equally crucial to recruit individuals based on their leadership potential and commitment to the organization's mission, rather than solely their corporate stature.

By recruiting individuals who we genuinely want and need, we maintain control over the composition of our board, ensuring a cohesive and effective leadership team. *(Secret)* Never recruit board members to appease them! There's an old axiom that says to keep our friends close and our enemies closer. This may be true, but it doesn't mean putting them above us in a position of power. This is a common mistake for newer executives. It always appears to be the easy way around a troubling volunteer, but it is exactly the

PLAYING BY THE RULES

opposite. If they're troubling now, just wait until they have power.

Cultivating Engagement and Ownership

Boards need to challenge their members to actively participate in organization initiatives. This involves not only approving projects but also committing to their execution. Implementing a dual voting system that gauges both support for initiatives and willingness to participate can incentivize board members to take ownership of their decisions. After all, in the grand theater of organization governance, board members should be more than mere spectators; they should be star performers, shining brightly as ambassadors for the organization. They should embody its values, not just recite them from memory, and actively contribute to its success, not just applaud from the audience.

So, let's encourage them to embrace their roles with gusto, because in this show, everyone has a part to play, and every contribution counts toward a standing ovation-worthy performance. Recruiting and engaging board members effectively are vital aspects of chamber management. By adopting proactive recruitment strategies, aligning board composition with organization goals, and upholding a culture of participation and accountability, chambers can cultivate dynamic and impactful leadership teams. The strength of a chamber lies in the collective commitment and dedication of its leaders.

As we noted earlier that the greatest characteristic of the best board members is that they make the chamber their first priority while they are on the chamber board, the next most important attributes to cultivate are preparedness and commitment.

A chamber's commitment to professionalism and excellence can be reflected in a strong, mandatory board orientation for all new members. By providing comprehensive training on roles, responsibilities, and organizational goals, the chamber will set the stage for board members to hit the ground running. This investment in onboarding will pay dividends in board cohesion and effectiveness, laying the groundwork for future success.

As recommended with new chamber member orientation, that first board orientation meeting with your newly elected board members also needs to say, this organization means business.

There's nothing like consistency in chamber orientations. That first meeting with newly elected board members should leave a dynamic impression. If your office boardroom is less than impressive, reach out to your corporate members on the board and ask to use their corporate boardroom. The most professional environment you can find will leave the most professional impression on those about to begin serving.

If there isn't a corporate boardroom available to you, consider an evening "Fireside Orientation" at the most elegant home you can find available to you. Veteran board members or highly supportive veteran volunteers can often help set this stage.

Environments have powerful first impressions and they make the orientation material all the more important; especially to those new board members thinking they were just going to occupy a seat. It's worth the extra effort and you just may find more veteran board members attending to support the presentation and making an even greater impression.

By leveraging the resources of corporate partners, the chamber can host orientation sessions in prestigious settings, instilling a sense of pride and importance in new board members. This strategic approach not only sets a positive tone for board engagement but also strengthens relationships with key stakeholders.

Shaping Boardroom Culture

The concept of viewing the board as an "Ensemble of Commerce" offers a fresh perspective on collaborative leadership and collective impact. Just as musicians in an ensemble harmonize their individual talents to create beautiful music, board members can leverage their diverse skills and backgrounds to drive organization success for us. By emphasizing collaboration over individualism, boards can unlock synergies and maximize their collective effectiveness.

(Secret) Encouraging boards to function as ensembles underscores the importance of teamwork, communication, and mutual respect. Like members of an orchestra, board members must synchronize their efforts and support one another to achieve common goals. Boards can transform into dynamic ensembles capable of orchestrating meaningful change and innovation within the organization. Utilizing music is always a great metaphor for defining what we want in developing leadership teams.

Openness to New Ideas

While building board dynamics, it's easy to fall into the trap of focusing solely on problems rather than solutions. This tendency mirrors the media's penchant for sensationalizing crises while neglecting victories. Boards often find themselves fixated on the negatives, whether its analyzing membership declines or dissecting operational setbacks. However, this myopic approach detracts from the board's ability to celebrate successes and replicate them.

When presenting reports to the board, it's crucial to shift the spotlight onto the positives. Instead of dwelling on why members are leaving, emphasize why new members are joining. By redirecting the discussion towards achievements and opportunities, boards can build a culture of optimism and proactive problem-solving. While it's important to address challenges, it's equally important to prioritize discussions on successes and opportunities during board meetings.

Embracing curiosity is key to facilitating a culture of learning and growth within the boardroom. The story of a new board member who bravely admitted her lack of understanding serves as a poignant reminder that asking questions is a sign of intelligence, not weakness. A young board member was elected to serve not only for her position in her company, but for her bright and assertive personality. Five minutes into her first meeting, she raised her hand. The board chair called on her. She said, "I'm sorry, but I have no idea what we are talking about." The board chair quickly apologized and brought her up to speed and the meeting resumed.

Later, after the meeting in the parking lot, three board members approached her and said "Thank you! We didn't know what they were talking about either." Board members, chosen for their expertise and acumen, should feel empowered to seek clarity and understanding when faced with unfamiliar topics or concepts. The lesson is if one doesn't know what is going on, we can be assured two to three others don't know either.

Encouraging open dialogue and inquiry not only enriches board discussions but also cultivates a culture of mutual support and collaboration. Rather than fearing judgment or ridicule, board members should embrace the opportunity to learn from one another and contribute to collective knowledge. *(Secret)* By championing a culture where asking questions is encouraged and celebrated, boards can harness the full potential of their diverse talents and experiences.

PLAYING BY THE RULES

They Can't Learn Without Instruction

The first impression a board member must have, is a sense of seriousness and discipline about the organization. If we treat the bylaws, policies, procedures, and orientation casually, we can expect our volunteers to mirror our actions. And that starts with a full orientation to ensure that they know what is expected from their important commitment.

Additionally, the need for attendance rules demonstrates the chamber's commitment to operational excellence and organization efficiency. By maintaining a high level of board engagement, the chamber can more effectively advance its mission, achieve its strategic goals, and serve the needs of its members and the community at large.

If harsh attendance rules rub you wrong, focus on more dynamic board agendas featuring speakers on issues and topics that create an eager desire to attend. However, instituting a disciplined bylaw on attendance gives an organization teeth to take action when a board member stops attending. By implementing clear guidelines regarding attendance expectations, the chamber communicates to its board members the importance of their active participation in board activities and decision-making processes.

Keep Them Coming Back

Board retention can be summed up in a nutshell. They feel an alignment to the mission, respected, that their input is valuable, and that their time is well spent (and never wasted).

The first two ideas have been discussed in earlier sections. But this last idea is one that cannot be overstated. Engaging members today means embracing their time. *(Secret)* Just because we schedule an hour for a board meeting doesn't mean we have to fill it. The phrase here is "shave and get out of the bathroom." Yes, there are times when we want more discussion, especially at the annual budget meeting and ratifying the board planning session goals. Otherwise, if we are taking longer than an hour, we're probably doing committee work.

In the past, a one-hour meeting meant almost two hours of time to attend. It takes an average of 15 minutes to drive there, have the "One Hour" meeting, chit chat and blah, blah, blah, for 15 minutes, and then another 15 minutes to get back. Today, if we say it's a one-hour meeting we had better prove it and live up to it. When we tell members the meeting is from noon to one, they will find a way to fill it even though they did what they needed to do long before one o'clock.

If we teach our committee chairs and board chairs to create 30-minute agendas starting at a quarter after the hour and ending at a quarter till the next hour, they will naturally compress their discussion and fill that time as well. And they won't fill it with filler. They will fill it with the business at hand.

It requires a strong agenda with updated background on all the agenda items and then a meeting with motions and actions that need to be addressed. We can do this, even with those "you know who's" that love the time away from work. This culture of efficient meetings takes effort to execute, but it is so important that it is worth it to implement. Make one-hour meetings, one hour. Compress meetings into 30 minutes leaving two 15-minute segments to come and go. The next generation is demanding it.

… CHAMBER WORLD

Chapter Six

From Vision to Vitality

CHAMBER WORLD

FROM VISION TO VITALITY

In today's rapidly evolving business environment, the chamber of commerce must continuously chart a strategic course to set objectives for the opportunities that lie ahead. Setting a clear direction is not merely an exercise in planning; it's the basis on which we build our organization's future and by default, our community's economic future. This involves a thorough process of defining our vision and mission, ensuring both are not only inspirational, but also actionable.

In charting our course, the goal is always to transform the guiding principles of our vision and mission into tangible outcomes that drive growth, innovation, and member engagement. By embracing a proactive approach, we can anticipate changes, adapt to new trends, and maintain our relevance as the pivotal force for commerce in our community.

To achieve this relevance, we must engage in regular strategic planning, bringing together diverse perspectives from our board members, staff, and stakeholders. This collaborative effort ensures that our plans are reflective of the needs and aspirations of our members.

Strategic planning is more than setting goals; it's about creating a roadmap that aligns our resources, initiatives, and activities with our agreed upon primary vision. By creating a culture of ownership and accountability, we empower our leadership to take bold steps toward shared objectives.

In charting this course, we commit to continuous evaluation and adjustment, ensuring that we remain agile and responsive to the ever-changing business environment. Through this disciplined approach, we can lead with confidence, drive meaningful impact, and uphold our commitment to being the beacon of progress for our members.

Branding Strategy and Mission Statement

Branding our individual chambers has been a constant challenge. I can't remember facilitating a planning retreat when one or more board members didn't recommend a goal of establishing or re-establishing their brand.

Before diving into specific goals and tactics, it's essential to identify the core brand that our strategy will be built upon. A strong brand positions us as the central hub for business and community engagement. This involves defining what our chamber stands for, what makes us unique, and how we want to be perceived by our members and the community.

(Secret) Our brand should encapsulate our vision, mission, and values, serving as the foundation for all of our initiatives and communications. This cohesive branding effort ensures that our strategic actions are aligned and reinforce the same message, creating a strong, unified identity that resonates with our audience and drives engagement.

Branding ourselves as 'the business center' is a strong brand that appears to never stop working. All of us want to be 'the first call' for business or 'the first step' for business. For Holly Hill, Florida Chamber of Commerce, branding themselves as *The Center of GOOD Business* was simple, yet powerful. It communicates their vision, mission, and values in just five words making it easy to understand and engage with them.

(Secret) Likewise, we should engage in a branding process that involves input from members and stakeholders to create a brand that reflects our commitment to supporting every business in the chamber and again by

default, the community. Our communications, events, member services, and even our physical presence should consistently reinforce what our vision states. Marketing materials should prominently feature our vision, and our events should be designed to highlight and promote the value of chamber membership.

For example, the Greater Des Moines Partnership reframed itself from a *Chamber of Commerce* to a *Partnership* and used the airport code DSM USA, to create a cohesive and recognizable brand that captures their regional focus and economic development efforts. These two actions provided the perspective that they were not a traditional chamber and in utilizing the airport code in their brand, immediately demonstrated that transportation is taken seriously and is covered.

Des Moines demonstrates again that the four keys to economic development are transportation and education--education and transportation.

With this thinking, it's become a dynamic trend in chambers, associations, and national sport leagues to utilize airport codes as a key identifier in building their brands. By unifying their marketing materials, events, and communications under the recognizable DSM USA brand, they've increased visibility and effectiveness in promoting the area as a vibrant place to live, work, and do business.

Having a clear, memorable vision and mission statement is crucial. These statements should guide and challenge every activity or decision within the chamber. Let the audience know what we are meant to be through our vision, and then let the mission state what we are willing to do to become what we imagine.

By doing so, we establish a logical flow that helps our stakeholders understand our ultimate goals and how we plan to achieve them. A compelling vision statement like Dubuque, Iowa's "Every Business a Member" articulates that they want to be known for being indispensable so it's not just about setting lofty goals, it's about beginning a concrete plan to achieve and activate them. The strategic planning process starts with defining our vision and mission, but then making sure they are inspiring, concise, and easily remembered.

As we enter the next planning season, board members should consider if it is good enough just to be a *Chamber of Commerce* or is it time to become a *Chamber for Commerce?*

Will our next vision be *The Voice of Business* or *The Voice for Business*? I'm not suggesting one is right and the other wrong, just asking which vision statement would drive a more powerful plan? Where one can be reactive, the other must be proactive. From the beginning we have professed to be "The Voice *of* Business" and it still stands as our true north, but let's look at how one little word can change our meaning and our actions.

Being the Voice *of* Business allows us to fall back and be a reactionary organization just waiting to respond to others as opposed to being proactive. Basically, we find ourselves reacting to other agendas instead of promoting our own initiatives. On the other hand, if we choose to be the Voice *for* Business like they do at the Fulshear (TX) Regional Chamber 'For' Commerce it suggests that we are required to be proactive in promoting the business agenda(s) that support our members. *(Secret)* Words have meaning, and the little words can have a big impact on any vision or mission statement.

In this context, let's take inspiration from Dubuque, Iowa with their vision of "Every Business a Member." This vision is not just a statement; it's a rallying cry that permeates every aspect of their operations.

FROM VISION TO VITALITY

Membership is the bottom line; it's the ultimate barometer of a chamber's success. While they may never reach 100% membership, the vision of nirvana doesn't allow them to give up. It demands that all activities and initiatives support membership growth, ensuring alignment with this aggressive goal.

This bold vision challenges us to think creatively and strategically about how we can attract, engage, and retain members. It sets a high standard and inspires a relentless pursuit of excellence in everything they do. *(Secret)* By adopting an equally ambitious vision, we can drive meaningful growth and make a substantial impact on our business community.

Strategies to Gather Input

Consistent strategic planning is the backbone of a successful chamber. To implement effective strategic planning, we must start with paying attention. We must listen more closely to what people are saying.

Many casual conversations can offer strategic insights. *(Secret)* Keep a strategic note file handy to record the concepts or thoughts offered by the hundreds of people we meet and greet throughout the year and be sure to keep the persons' name next to the idea to offer credit later if needed.

No survey or suggestion box is more powerful than an executive's strategic planning notes, but we can multiply this planning approach by asking staff members to do the same by paying closer attention to what people are saying in their circles. *(Secret)* Make it a staff meeting agenda item under "What I heard" and don't just look for the positives, write down the negatives as well. Strategic information hides in all communication.

Paying attention to local media is equally critical, especially in how the media treats your chamber of commerce. Paying attention to popular local podcasts and, of course, social media will often give us a pulse of the community on a larger scale.

Next, listening to, and paying attention to, the chamber's information director offers front desk insights that impact planning, as well as day-to-day operations. Here is a person who knows... everything. This person is the Alpha and Omega of every chamber, every association, and every business that employs a front desk.

Think about that for a moment, this person sees everyone who enters and everyone who leaves. This person knows who's happy and who's not happy. And they usually know why. Sadly, it's the person we have historically paid the least who seems to know the most. We need to change that going forward.

(Secret) As for seeking feedback through member surveys, it's worth repeating; never ask "How are we doing?" The reason is, they don't really know. The majority of board members don't really know unless it's a board meeting day and they're paying attention. The best way to find out 'how we are doing' is to tell them with a bulleted list featuring a margin for grading. This strategy is 1) your survey, and 2) additional marketing of what the chamber is doing. Two birds. One stone.

The Planning Retreat

A clever name for the annual retreat is by calling it an *advance planning session.* A planning retreat or an advance, are basically taking one step backward to take two steps forward so for some, naming the retreat an 'advance' underscores where you want the meeting to take you.

Building a comprehensive plan involves board members, committee chairs, who are often left out, staff members, and key stakeholders who are usually our major sponsors and financial partners. The purpose is to create a focused environment where we can review past performance, assess current challenges, and set clear objectives for the future. The planning session is a learning session for new board members and other new participants as it requires open dialogue, encourages diverse perspectives, and promotes collaborative problem-solving. By doing so, we ensure that our strategic and tactical plans are well-represented and reflective of the collective insights and expertise within our chamber's membership.

A crucial aspect of successful strategic planning is establishing a sense of authorship and ownership among all participants. This can be achieved by involving a broad range of stakeholders in the planning process. By soliciting input from various members, we can ensure that our plans are comprehensive and inclusive. This approach not only enhances the quality of the plans but also builds a strong sense of commitment and hopefully, accountability by the participants.

Terminology can help direct our thinking toward planning. Conducting what could be termed an X-Ray Analyses of our programs and events while planning helps participants remain engaged and aligned with our strategic goals. An X-ray, in this context, means looking through our operations to identify areas that may be cracked, broken, or dislocated.

When stakeholders feel that they have contributed to the development of the plan, they are more likely to support and advocate for its implementation. *(Secret)* When more people are involved in crafting the plan, they become more invested in its success. The adage, if they write the plan, they will underwrite the plan, perfectly sums up this philosophy.

Aside from the obvious people who attend chamber planning sessions, inviting the marketing directors of our corporate sponsors, if we can't get the chief executive officer, helps ensure longer term sponsor relationships by allowing them equal authorship of when, where, and how their money is going to be spent. It's difficult not to underwrite a plan the sponsor helped to write.

Another successful strategy was proven when the Birmingham Business Alliance (BBA) in Alabama transformed their planning process by engaging a broad range of stakeholders, including business leaders, educational institutions, and community organizations where they had great success and even greater ownership.

This inclusive approach helped the BBA to create a comprehensive economic development strategy that focused on key areas such as workforce development, innovation, and regional collaboration. Authorship does create ownership.

<u>Turning Thoughts into Plans</u>

I was never a fan of the "strengths, weaknesses, opportunities, threats (S.W.O.T.) planning analysis"[2] because it typically ended meetings on a negative note. Strengths and Weaknesses help identify opportunities but concluding with Threats left people focused on problems rather than on goals. So, I rearranged the letters to SWTO for my meeting agendas, but it made a terrible acronym.

That's when I created my own Ex.L.A.R.G.E. planning agenda featuring **Ex**pectations, **L**ove, **A**bsences, **R**oadblocks, **G**oals, and **E**xecution of those goals. This new framework not only restructured the planning process but also injected a positive, goal-oriented approach to strategic discussions,

---

[2] The original SWOT analysis, called the SOFT approach (Stewart et al., 1965a, p. 16), was designed as a tool in one of the earliest strategic planning frameworks, named the System of Plans (Stewart, 1963).

ensuring that the focus remained on actionable outcomes.

As I considered this, all my planning sessions began with participants sharing their expectations of the meetings outcome, so in my acronym, I listed Ex first. The "L"; was for creating a Love list of everything that members and volunteers currently loved about the organization which defined our strengths in a positive exercise. Next, instead of asking about what is weak, which felt too negative, I would ask, "What's Absent?" meaning what's missing or what aren't we doing that we should be doing? This gave a positive look at the negative in the planning process.

When I redefined threats as roadblocks it created a metaphor asking, "What's stopping us from moving forward?" This approach encouraged a more constructive dialogue where participants naturally flowed their thinking by first identifying gaps and obstacles which then became opportunities for improvement. Goals sums up and supports items on the first four letters and execution lists and prioritizes what, when and who will make sure the goals get done.

Here's a picture of how this Ex.L.A.R.G.E. planning agenda flows:

Ex. = Expectations are the Alpha and Omega of planning. They set the direction of every session and then challenge the outcomes at the end when evaluating if the outcomes matched the expectations listed.

L. = Love list. Listing what we love about the chamber including our programs, events, committees, and operations is always inspiring…until someone says, "Yeah but, look what we aren't doing…"

A. = Absent. Instead of listing weaknesses, we ask, "What's missing or What aren't we doing that we should be doing? This is a more intense and eye-opening conversation…Until someone says, "Here's <u>why</u> we aren't doing this or that…

R. = Roadblocks? Participants are given six overarching reasons why certain things are missing: Time, Money, Fear, Pride, Politics, and Communication. Those discussion topics reveal deeper truths under those six common obstacles…Finally someone will say, "Then all we need to do is…"

G. = Goals? Planning goals usually support what's on the Love list and fills the voids under the 'Absent' list to overcome the Roadblocks. The Roadblocks define why and where the problems are, and the Goals become our objectives in overcoming those things that are missing.

E. = Execution. This is where we list what needs to be done, when it needs to be done and who is going to do it...We stop when someone says, "LET'S PARTY!" and celebrate another great planning retreat.

Start Counting Your Coincidences

(Secret) Writing down our goals is a powerful practice that transforms vague aspirations into concrete plans. By putting our goals on paper, we create a tangible reminder of what we aim to achieve, making it easier to stay focused and motivated. This practice also allows us to track our progress and celebrate milestones along the way. By being constantly aware of our goals, we become more attuned to opportunities and coincidences that can help us achieve them.

You are reading a goal that has been on my list for years. Had it not stayed on my list we would not be having this interaction. Goals change everything, and goals are much more achievable when we understand how goal setting works.

Goal setting is a lot like buying a new car. Two things happen when we buy a new car, even if the new car is a used car, the same two things happen when we buy it; number 1) we lose money the moment we drive it off the car lot, because every car starts depreciating once we buy it. Number 2) everywhere we drive we start seeing the same car we just bought. It doesn't matter if you buy a Maserati or a Mazda, wherever you go you will see the same car you've just purchased and for a while, you'll even see the old car you traded in. To understand why this happens is to understand how goal setting works.

In a word, the answer is awareness. We can't help but be aware of the new car we're driving. We're in it every day. We own it! We look at it every day. How can we not be aware of others that look just like it? Goal setting works the same way.

A great mentor of mine taught me to take the time to not only write out my goals on a yellow legal pad, but to look at them every day, no matter how little I had done in achieving them. If I wrote them down and constantly reviewed them, he said I would own them and once I owned them, only then could I start counting my coincidences. What? Counting my coincidences? Yes, he said, coincidences. Coincidences are the opportunities that support and begin fulfilling our goals. Like a new car, opportunities are the other cars we start to notice when we buy one.

FROM VISION TO VITALITY

This book was a goal and Lory Mitchell Wingate, my publisher was my great coincidence as she invited me to the book writing world at the time in my career that I was ready to write. Because of her, you are reading my little tirade of secrets and opinions of our Chamber World, he said with a wink and a smile.

Buy into your goals and own them by looking at them once a day. This often requires forcing yourself to look at them, because you're embarrassed that you haven't done anything to achieve them... yet. Keep looking and stay aware.

Planning Roadblocks

(Secret) If we can't afford to have a planning session, it tells us the last one failed. If our board feels we can't afford to hold a planning session, that should be the principal reason in arguing for one. If we're broke, the cheapest thing we can do is go back to the drawing board. If we're broke and don't come up with a new plan, we can plan on staying broke by default. Whether it's board planning, a potential member joining or continuing education for staff, the real cost is always found in whether we do it or don't do it.

An additional roadblock to strategic planning is the word itself; strategic. Does anyone have the actual definition at hand? Along with vision and mission, the word *strategic* often intimidates planning participants who aren't involved in organized planning on a regular basis. They're not sure what it means or if they are even qualified to participate.

Remove the roadblock by taking the time to define a strategic plan as setting a long-term vision for various strategic areas of your organization. Then let them know the session will include tactical planning which will be the creation of actionable goals and objectives, or what is commonly called a Program of Work. The strategic plan will guide the organization between three and five years while the tactical Program of Work reflects the strategic plan with goals to be achieved in one to three years.

Adaptation and Innovation

Leadership often requires making bold decisions and setting a new direction. *(Secret)* Removing old symbols or practices that no longer serve the organization's future can signify a fresh start and a forward-looking vision. This act demonstrates your commitment to innovation and progress, encouraging others to embrace change and

FROM VISION TO VITALITY

focus on future opportunities. This decisive action can have a profound impact, signaling to the organization that it's time to move forward.

Rich Hadley was an icon in the chamber of commerce industry and past president and Chief Executive Officer of the Spokane, Washington Chamber, which is now GSI, Greater Spokane Incorporated. In physical stature only, I stood taller than Rich, but there was never a moment when I didn't look up to him. I remember him as the consummate chamber of commerce executive and someone I could only wish to emulate.

When Rich replaced the retiring George Reitemeier, another iconic leader, I couldn't help but feel bad for him. Historically, when an executive steps in and replaces a 20+ year successful chief executive officer, it usually becomes an interim position, but not with Rich Hadley. I was a Rich Hadley fan before I met him. A staff member of the Spokane Chamber that I knew told me Rich was taking a tour of the Chamber offices with his new team when they entered the Chamber lobby lined with old photographs of past Chamber presidents that had been up there forever. Rich looked up and said, "Take them down..."

A shocked staff member asked, "Can we do that?!?" That's when Rich established his leadership, "From this moment on, this organization is looking forward, not backward."

I'll never forget the impact this story and Rich Hadley had on me. And I still hadn't met him! We didn't have past presidents or chairmen on our walls next door in Coeur d'Alene, but we had a ton of old photographs and memories that made us look like a museum, not a chamber of commerce. They all came down immediately and went into an album that's probably lost and forgotten by now.

Then I looked at my own office and saw my "ego wall" with awards and plaques that were earned five, ten, and even fifteen years earlier and thought, "What in the world am I doing looking backwards?" They all came down as well and I challenged myself to refill that wall with new plaques.

"Take them down." A simple statement created a powerful future by breaking from the past and inspiring a culture of forward thinking. By setting a clear, forward direction, we can lead organizations toward a more dynamic and successful future, just as Rich Hadley did for Spokane.

FROM VISION TO VITALITY

The chamber of commerce must continuously reimagine its roles and responsibilities, and leaders must think creatively. It's no longer enough to maintain the status quo; we must innovate and adapt to meet member expectations. This requires a willingness to take risks and try new ideas, even if some may fail. The essence of our success lies in our ability to evolve with the times, ensuring that our offerings remain relevant and progressive. As Peter Drucker said, "If you want something new, you have to stop doing something old."

By embracing a mindset of continuous improvement, we can create an environment that thrives on creativity—making us ready to tackle the challenges and seize the opportunities that come our way. Adapting our operations involves a thorough review and overhaul of our current programs and initiatives. We must be willing to let go of outdated practices and embrace new methodologies that align with our strategic goals. Introducing industry-specific training programs focused on emerging technologies, such as AI, blockchain, and digital marketing, can help members stay ahead of the curve.

Providing training on sustainable business practices and green certifications supports member efforts towards corporate social responsibility. Developing or expanding leadership boot camps and mentorship programs nurture the next generation of business leaders.

Launching initiatives focused on corporate social responsibility can also build upon our value. Developing a certification program to recognize businesses that excel in social responsibility incentivizes higher ethical practices. Promoting Green programs that encourage recycling, energy efficiency, and sustainable practices among member businesses supports environmental stewardship. Clean and Green initiatives go much farther when done together with a professional leadership organization like the chamber of commerce.

Think outside of the...

If you aren't thinking "box" right now, you must live in another country. Here in the U.S., thinking outside of the box is such a worn-out cliché, I got tired of rolling my eyes, so I started using a Pacific Northwest variable for reminding audiences to think outside of *the forest*.

When we live and work in a 'forest,' all the trees represent all those issues, problems, and opportunities we face every day in the

FROM VISION TO VITALITY

Chamber World. Some of us are surrounded by large Sequoia type trees while most are surrounded by hundreds of tall skinny pine trees taking up our days.

In our 'forests,' it's almost impossible to see beyond the trees that surround us, that is until a helicopter drops a cable, and hoists us out of our forest and gently lands us upon a hill where we can turn around, look, and see *all* the trees that make up our entire forest.

Every time you and I attend a national, regional, or statewide conference, we are metaphorically going there to stand on a hill to look beyond the local trees that surround us every day to see how the rest of the world is doing. Not only do the conference seminars enlighten us, but the other *Chamber World* foresters are there as well to cajole, commiserate, and share their problems along with their solutions. Learning those solutions pays for the entire expense in attending and then some. Always ask yourself what it will cost if you don't go to these dynamic meetups.

Have you ever noticed the word *learning* contains the word *earning*? I can't begin to tell you how many excellent concepts and ideas I learned from other executives and applied, resulting in earnings of literally thousands of dollars for the different chambers of commerce

I served. But the greatest idea and concept was born in my own mind while standing on a hill at the U.S. Chamber of Commerce Institute for Organization Management.

Most if not all chambers of commerce began with utilizing what is called a "Fair Share" membership rate card. If a member had one to three employees, membership was at its lowest level. As employee counts increased, membership rates rose accordingly. The thinking was if a business could afford to hire two employees, they could easily afford to join at the two-employee rate. If a business hired ten employees, a higher price was deemed acceptable. For some, when business was tough, this system forced people to lie. Even a board member gave me a much lower count of employees than I knew was true.

I was stymied. How could we get honest numbers from our members? Then I went back to Institute with this tree in my forest looming over me. I asked many of my colleagues and no one could offer anything to help except to say, "They all do it, let it go." That wasn't true either. They didn't *all* do it, but many did. I remained stymied but focused on finding an answer.

My next class at the Institute was an elective to learn about the Microsoft Access®

software program that many chambers were using at the time. As I sat behind the computer screen, I watched as the program logo slowly loaded and began coming up on the screen. THERE IT WAS! My answer to the problem. It was ACCESS!

With the fair share dues system, we didn't have an avenue for successful members to pay us more and obviously, we didn't have anything to offer those members who were struggling to make ends meet. *(Secret)* Our members needed THEIR access to the chamber, not ours. I immediately switched over to Microsoft Word® and developed the first tiered dues program in the nation. We called it "Membership Access" and rolled it out the following January and increased membership income by $44,000 that first year.

Tiered dues have evolved since then, but the point here is that I needed to get out of my forest allowing me to open my eyes wider so I could see all the trees in finding a solution. If you can't get to Institute or an industry conference, take a walk. Just get out and start thinking outside of your forest.

Adapting to change by adding new programs that align with a new branding strategy would also add excitement and generate renewed interest in the organization by both volunteers and staff members.

Creating incubator and accelerator programs can further support our members. Establishing a plan with incubator spaces for startups, providing members with office space, mentorship, and access to funding, furthers innovation and entrepreneurship. Setting up innovation labs where businesses can collaborate on projects, share resources, and test new ideas promotes a culture of continuous improvement which can be driven by any chamber wanting to build their value.

The Greater Louisville Inc. (GLI) provides an excellent case study of successfully adapting and innovating to meet member needs. GLI implemented a strategic plan focusing on talent development, innovation, and regional economic growth. They launched the "Live in Lou" initiative, which aims to attract and retain talent in the Louisville region by showcasing the area's quality of life and career opportunities.

Additionally, GLI's "Advantage Louisville" program focuses on innovation and entrepreneurship through incubators, mentorship, and funding opportunities for startups. These initiatives have significantly contributed to the economic vitality of the

Louisville region and have strengthened GLI's role as a catalyst for business growth, proving that GLI steps up to the plate and goes to bat for their members and community.

Ultimately, the journey of reimagining and adapting our operations is one of ongoing transformation. It requires us to remain open to feedback, continuously evaluate our impact, and be daring in our vision for the future. Regular feedback mechanisms, such as surveys and polls, help gather member insights on various aspects of the chamber's operations. Organizing focus groups allows us to delve deeper into specific issues and gather detailed feedback. Implementing digital and physical suggestion boxes ensures we capture ideas and feedback from members at any time.

By taking these steps, we can ensure that our chambers remain at the forefront of innovation and adaptation, meeting the evolving needs of our members and leading our business community towards a prosperous future. Let's take inspiration from the GLI, BBA, and DSM USA initiatives and carry forward this spirit of reinvention into every aspect of our chamber's work, ensuring that we not only meet but exceed the expectations of our business community.

Evolving the chamber of commerce and executing a successful strategy requires reimagining our operations, engaging in regular strategic planning, aligning our vision and mission, while adapting to constant market changes. By charting a clear course and following it diligently, we can make certain that the chamber remains relevant, impactful, and indispensable to our members. We do this to keep leading, innovating, and striving to be a chamber of commerce and a force for business.

Operationalizing the Vision and Mission

Once the vision and mission are established, they should be embedded into the chamber's operations and its culture. Consistently include the vision and mission statements in all communications, such as newsletters, social media posts, and event materials. Some chambers even include the vision and mission within their logos.

Embedding our vision and mission in our communications can't help but influence operational behavior toward success. Evaluate all programs and initiatives to ensure they align and support the vision and mission. Discontinue or modify any activities that do not support these core statements and that all staff members and volunteers understand and can articulate the vision and mission when asked about the chamber. Always emphasize the importance of these statements and how they guide daily operations in orientations for new members and in new board member orientations. Display the vision and mission statements prominently in your office, on your website, and at all events. This constant visibility keeps them top-of-mind for everyone involved with the chamber of commerce.

Monitoring and reinforcing the relevance of the vision and mission is also essential. Conduct regular reviews to ensure these statements remain aligned with the evolving goals of the chamber. Adjust them as necessary to reflect changes in the business environment. These statements were written on paper, not in stone.

Develop performance metrics that measure progress towards the vision and adherence to the mission. Metrics include membership growth, event attendance, and the success of advocacy efforts.

Celebrate milestones and achievements that align with the vision and mission. Recognize and reward volunteers, members, and staff who contribute significantly to these goals. Establish mechanisms for ongoing feedback from members and stakeholders on how well the chamber is living up to its vision and mission. Use this feedback to make continuous improvements.

I understand how redundant I'm being here. I also understand that repetition is the key to memory, but then again, repetition is the key to memory. If the vision and mission of our chamber of commerce isn't our mantra and isn't easily repeated when people ask what we do, then we may as well not have either.

Chapter Seven

The Good Leader

CHAMBER WORLD

THE GOOD LEADER

Leadership skills sustain organization vitality and propels community development. Effective leaders within a chamber must not only possess the ability to inspire and motivate staff and volunteer teams but also facilitate the moods and movements of member needs, economic trends, civic engagement, all while driving the board's strategic initiatives. Leadership in this context is about more than just guiding an organization, it's about being visionary looking beyond the present challenges and tackling opportunities right in front of us.

Throughout my career, I have focused on paying attention and knowing what's going on around me. This situational awareness, as well as the visionary aspects required to lead, remains the foundation of developing specific skills for leading and managing in the *Chamber World*.

Influence and Presence

Leaders, specifically chamber leaders, must have a sense of themselves in how important we are to every meeting we attend. Be careful. This isn't to build our ego, it's to reflect how important our organization, the chamber of commerce, is to others who attend the meetings we are invited to.

I've never been the smartest guy in the room, but often felt I was the most confident. I didn't know all the answers, but in my role, it was my job to know who did have the answers. People knew that I would know who did know, silly as that may sound. It gave me a sense that people were thinking, *"The chamber is here, now the meeting can begin,"* and I did my best to underscore that thinking. Again, this was not out of conceit or ego, it was about reflecting how important the connections we have in the chamber that are critical to the success of our organizations and community.

Influence and presence are not just desirable traits, they are essential for success. The great compliment for people with true presence is that they *turn on the lights without touching a switch.* One person can fill the room with their presence, and I am always attracted to them. We can only hope others feel the same about us, and to make that happen, we must put the focus on our strengths, not our weaknesses.

Our greatest strength in the *Chamber World* is found in our connections or nexus. *(Secret)* It's our unspoken mission of doing together what we can't do alone. It was always my role to facilitate those connections which multiplied my value, not to mention my influence creating a sense of confidence in me, and therefore a sense of confidence in the chamber of commerce.

Chamber executives often want to be humble by saying, "I'm not the chamber, our members are the chamber." While this may be true, it's not what is perceived. If you are the chief executive officer or executive director, then you are perceived to be the chamber of commerce and if something is perceived, it might as well be accepted as true. They see us as the Chamber so we must give them the very best perception with every interaction, unapologetically.

This sense of presence and influence gives us the ability to mold opinions, guide decisions, and inspire action. A chamber leader's presence must command, or at the very least, invite attention to set the tone for engagement among members and stakeholders. Once earned, our influence drives the strategic initiatives that propel our missions.

In the *Chamber World*, we strive to continuously tell our story and keep members and the public informed. We do this through a variety of platforms including online monthly newsletters, weekly updates, all the way up to our annual reports, many of which get lost in the volume of messages we send. We find ourselves constantly telling our story without thinking about or paying attention to our member's story.

As much as I wanted others to read my newsletters, especially my monthly 'CEO column,' I found myself skipping over and tossing away newsletters that our members, including our important corporate members, would send the chamber as a courtesy. I was treating their publications the way I was sure they were treating ours. It was then I realized a hard truth; we're not that important to them. Of course, we're important when they need us, but otherwise, we're not the priority we imagine ourselves to be.

Maybe, just maybe I thought, if I started reading their newsletters, I could understand better what is important to them and re-focus my columns on their issues instead of mine. After all, the number #1 rule in business is, *you get what you give,* so I gave it a shot, and I was surprised with the response after quoting a prominent chief executive officer and chamber member in my column. They still passed over our newsletter until someone mentioned that I quoted them. Our relationships quickly became more important, and we started paying more attention to each other.

An obvious as well as additional benefit to paying closer attention to our members' publications was the genius they had to offer. Hecla Mining Company is a worldwide corporation headquartered in Coeur d'Alene, Idaho. Art Brown was their Chief Executive Officer and while I initially only interacted with his team who would represent the company on our committees and board of directors, things changed when I quoted Art from a brilliant monthly column he authored, encouraging all his employees to, "Ask the CEO."

What Does a CEO Do?

A Hecla miner working in South America came up with a question most employees were afraid to ask, *"What the Hell does a CEO do?"* Art began his career in the mines and congratulated his fellow miner for having the courage to ask the question and his answer was so profound that I have since shared it with thousands of audience members in leadership classes coast to coast. *(Secret)* Art began by writing, "A CEO works twenty years from now, while a chief operating officer works in the here and now."

He was brief and brilliant as he went on to explain that when you see him with his feet on the desk looking out the window, he's planning for the next twenty years so our children will have a place in the company, and when he's on the golf course with other chief executive officer's, they're all talking about the future, not about a hook or a slice.

A chief executive officer is a strategic position while a chief operating officer position is tactical. One is a leader while the other is a manager. This reflected perfectly the lesson taught at the Institute for Organization Management, "Leaders do the right thing, and managers do things right." Art gave it real life meaning and while regretting all the past newsletters I passed over; I seldom missed another one.

As I began reading the Hecla Mining newsletters, I became more supportive of the environmental issues they were mitigating and fighting due to past mining issues that depleted the fishery in Lake Coeur d'Alene. That year, I was on vacation in Washington

D.C. and walked by the filthy basin next to the Thomas Jefferson Memorial with dead and dying fish floating to the top. I couldn't help but write my own newsletter article entitled, "Dead fish lapping at the feet of Thomas Jefferson" reminding the federal government that they should take care of their own fish as well. We became more important to Art and his company.

(Secret) Being successful in our *Chamber Worlds* requires looking inside other worlds. It's an ideal strategy when we want the true pulse of our membership. Their interests, wants, and needs become obvious when we walk a mile in their shoes by perusing their newsletters, press releases and bulletins.

Nearly 70% of Communication is Non-verbal

Advocacy is a crucial aspect of chamber leadership, but it doesn't always require words. Your presence alone in this arena of issues and local politics can be a powerful statement. Government meetings, while often long and tedious, are necessary for ensuring that your members' voices are represented. Simply showing up can make a significant impact, demonstrating your commitment to representing your organizations' interests.

CHAMBER WORLD

Sitting quietly in the front row can be more powerful than speaking. Elected officials and council members will always notice your presence and wonder about your intentions, giving you an edge. Non-verbal cues, such as an attentive listening pose with strategic head nods or shakes, can communicate your stance effectively, especially when the opposition is at the lectern pontificating their points of view. This silent form of advocacy can be surprisingly influential, proving again that sometimes, less is more.

This is one of the most important lessons for new executives in a chamber of commerce who have no background or training in government relations or politics. *(Secret)* You don't have to say a word, simply look approving when you approve and look concerned when you disagree. Once you become more adept, you will find yourself nodding imperceptibly when you support an issue and slightly shaking your head when expressing disagreement. I can't begin to tell you how powerful this is, especially when you take your seat in the front row.

<u>The Seat of Power Is Furthest from The Door.</u>

C.A.V.E. PEOPLE. We all have them: **C**itizens **A**gainst **V**irtually **E**verything. These are often people who like things just the way they are and to them, progress is a pariah. They seem to get in the way of everything we're trying to do. The frustration they create is palpable, which usually results in argument and anger. It was Eleanor Roosevelt who taught us that anger is one letter away from danger. CAVE People are usually highly intelligent and come to meetings armed with a well-prepared position, and advanced communications skills that strengthen their argument.

CAVE People make a conspicuous entrance as they walk into the room bringing along their negative aura and always sit in the front row commanding full attention of the city council, county commissioners, or state legislators they are trying to convince. Alternatively, chamber of commerce executives or government affairs volunteers usually sit in the middle or back rows where they become invisible to the elected officials. We've lost before we started.

(Secret) Before ever disagreeing with your opponents, go to school on them. You'll quickly learn they already know the seat of power in any meeting is furthest from the door and always the front row facing authority. They already know there is power in numbers and invite their members to sit with them and we don't.

Allowing your opponents to impress you will help suppress your anger and encourage you to focus on beating them at their own game. Sitting next to a CAVE person in a city council meeting is like sitting in someone's pew at church, it's disconcerting to them and creates a moment to inwardly smile for us.

Body language, physical positioning, and making silence truly golden are strategic skills we must continually master in establishing our presence and influence in every leadership environment.

Disciplines of Chamber Leadership

Of all the disciplines leaders and managers must have to acquire success, the first discipline is to be disciplined. The *Chamber World* can often become comfortable or casual and therefore lax in its presentation, style, and overall image. If we're coasting, we have to be going downhill; simple physics demands it. We can't coast on a level plane. Coasting on a level plane is just coming to a slow stop. This is not the momentum we're trying to achieve.

For business, I'm a coat and tie guy. Always have been. Always will be. It's a generational thing. I still shine my shoes for crying out loud. I apologize, but I was taught that my level of dress reflected my level of respect for others. It was my own personal discipline. I always had to be ready for a surprise visit from the Governor, so I dressed as if everyone was the Governor. O.K., you, and mom are both right; clothes don't make the man, but sometimes they can unmake the man.

In a moment of weakness, my team convinced me to have a Casual Friday dress code. It wasn't long before Casual Friday became Gardening Friday and then the Governor came in. OK, it wasn't the Governor, but it was the most prominent businessman in our community that had never visited our office before. It wasn't pretty. I kept babbling an apology for the way we looked and after he left, I came up with a new dress code, Casual Saturday.

I'm not suggesting this be your discipline, especially in our casual, untucked world today. Being overdressed today is as uncomfortable for this generation as being underdressed was for my generation. My dress is my discipline because it works for me. I'm more confident being overdressed than I ever would be underdressed in representing my community.

Listening is a more difficult discipline. If you are a speed reader, the cliché of *two ears and one mouth, use them accordingly* is this message in a nutshell. Not talking is the hardest discipline for a personality like mine, and while I'm much better at listening and not talking today, it's a constant struggle. One lesson that has helped more than any other was learning that people like me listen to respond, and don't necessarily listen to hear the other person's entire thought.

Now, when I find myself wanting to jump in and interrupt the other person, I silently SCREAM these two words over and over in my mind, SHUT UP! SHUT UP! SHUT UP! Surprisingly, it works most of the time, but some disciplines take more practice than others.

Managing with Maslow

Abraham Maslow's hierarchy of human needs[3] has been a constant guide in my life as a leader and a manager. Just below our highest need for self-actualization, or being fulfilled in reaching our full potential, is self-esteem.

Self-esteem and conceit are often confused, but they are fundamentally different. Arrogance and conceit are masks for low self-esteem, whereas true self-esteem is grounded

---

[3] Maslow, A.H. (1943). A theory of human motivation. Psychological Review, 50, 370-396.

in self-respect and confidence. High self-esteem comes from recognizing your own worth and abilities without needing to belittle others or seek constant validation.

Leaders with high self-esteem more often focus on giving credit rather than seeking it. They derive fulfillment from the success of their team and organization, not from personal accolades. This approach creates a positive work environment and attracts people who are drawn to confident and secure leaders. *(Secret)* By establishing a culture focusing on the success of others, leaders can build a strong, cohesive organization. This is not to say these leaders don't focus on themselves, as constant self-improvement is a critical expertise in leading and managing others.

Self-improvement is a continuous journey that reflects our commitment to personal and professional growth. *(Secret)* Reflecting on what we have done recently to better ourselves is a crucial practice. Whether it's acquiring new skills, reading insightful books, or adopting healthier habits, these actions demonstrate a proactive approach to our self-development.

In professional interactions like a job interview, being able to articulate your recent self-improvement efforts can set us apart. It shows that we are not complacent and are always striving to enhance our capabilities. This mindset not only benefits you personally but also positively impacts your organization by bringing fresh perspectives and skills to the table.

Greatest Interview I Ever Failed

I absolutely loved my early career in broadcasting, until I didn't. I needed more purpose in life than playing music and telling jokes. That's when I found the chamber of commerce, or should I say the chamber found me. Being a young chamber exec had its perks like playing golf with highly successful local business leaders. While in the Lakewood, Washington Chamber, I was invited to play in a tournament with the chairman of a large group of radio stations. We had a great time and he suggested I get back into the radio business, so he set up an interview for me.

Not thinking about going back, but I was flattered by the invitation and the potential pay increase, so I went to the interview with the station's general manager. I was breezing through the interview with questions about broadcasting, but then he asked a personal question I wasn't prepared for..."*Pat, what have you done recently to improve yourself?*"

THE GOOD LEADER

After losing 75 pounds the year before and having begun a lifelong goal of reading a book a month, for some reason those didn't come to mind. I didn't see those things as self-improvement as much as they were self-preservation and self-enjoyment, so I stumbled and said, "Uh... apply for this job?"

I literally watched him take his pen to the top of his notes and scratch me off his list even though his boss set up our interview. He gave me the courtesy of five more minutes and walked me to the door. I knew I had failed and immediately went to school on what just happened.

Here's what I came up with; why would a company always trying to improve itself hire anyone who isn't trying to improve himself or herself? I failed the interview but forwarded the question to my calendar on January first of every year to review my new answers. I also kept the question for future interviews with potential employees of my own and to take it a step further, *'What Have You Done Recently to Improve Yourself'* also became an agenda item at annual staff retreats so everyone would be prepared to answer the question again and again.

(Secret) Make self-improvement a habit and demonstrate that behavior. This takes work

and self-awareness. Your effort to improve yourself inspires all around you. There is no momentum on a level plane. Great leaders are always striving to learn, and improvements are always a step up.

Leading Through Wisdom Found

In the beginning as a young executive, I didn't think of joining the chamber that hired me, but only because I was a young executive. Joining the chamber of commerce that you lead can be a powerful first move. It shows your commitment to the organization and sets a positive example for others. When board members see that you have joined, it reinforces your dedication and can inspire others to join or renew their membership.

Every job in business has some personal expense to incur, but this one always seemed to pay for itself when an unhappy member would begin a tirade with, "I'm a member of this Chamber and I want…" It was the perfect reply to cool their jets when I would say, "I'm a member too."

For membership directors, being a member of the chamber allows you to speak from personal experience. You can share why you joined and the benefits you've received, making your sales pitch more authentic and compelling. This approach not only builds credibility but also demonstrates your belief in the value of the organization you represent. "Do as I say, not as I do," is a weak position to hold in any leadership role.

Five Appearances of Leadership

Whether we believe it or not, how we show up is how we are perceived. It makes a difference, and we need to pay attention to it. When we think about how we want to be perceived, we can focus on a few key areas such as, are we a member ourselves, are we dressing the part, are we behaving as expected for our role as a chamber of commerce leader.

Appearance #1: Appear

The first lesson in board orientation is reminding board members that 80% of their job is simply showing up. The other 20% is standing up and speaking up for the chamber. Some board members will ask, "What if I have nothing to say?" and my response is always, "Awesome! Shorter meetings!" But then I ask, "What if an issue comes up that negatively impacts your business or your industry?" Please show up.

For the chamber executive and staff, my rule was for all of us to be working at 8:00 a.m., not showing up at 8:00 a.m. It's hard to be open or answer the phone while we're hanging up our jackets or pouring coffee. It's hard to have presence or influence if we don't appear and appear on time.

Appearance #2: Appear Healthy

Healthy body, healthy mind. A healthy mind wants a healthy body. We need to make health a priority in every office encouraging healthy food, drinking plenty of water, taking a walk (especially helpful during a crisis when possible) and building camaraderie with office softball or pickleball teams. Meet with a human resource professional to identify the current rules and regulations to promote any business health program.

Appearance #3: Appear Knowledgeable

Know your stuff. Challenge every employee, including the chief executive officer to cross-train at the reception desk for a minimum of four hours once a year. We are the information center for the entire community. This is everyone's job in *Chamber World*. Have fun with it. Challenge everyone to answer the phone with, "*MyTown* Chamber, we can help you!" We don't have to have all the knowledge, but as mentioned earlier, we just need to know who would know. If we know that, we can live up to our promise every time we answer the phone.

Appearance #4: Appear interested

People who appear interested appear as if they care. Focus on the people at hand and let voice mail keep your attention on the person you're with. The more interest we show in others, especially in person, the more interest they will show in us. Often, we have to multi-task with three or more people in line. This is a problem every business wants! Take advantage of it with the way you recognize all people in line while taking care of them one at a time.

Appearance #5: Appear professional

No. I'm not here to tell you how to dress. I am here to recommend each of us figure out how we want to appear in representing the business community and our city. *(Secret)* Does our dress ethic match our work ethic? The way we dress in a professional setting can significantly impact perceptions and performance. While dress codes provide someone else's guidelines, our own dress ethic reflects our individual understanding of the professional environment and our level of respect for it. It's essential, however, to dress in a way that aligns with our organization's mission and the expectations of our roles.

If unsure about the importance of dress in your professional life, try a simple experiment. Choose your best business outfit and wear it to work without mentioning it to anyone. Observe how you feel and how others react. Often, dressing up can boost our confidence and change the way we are perceived by colleagues. At the end of the day, reflect on whether the experience was positive or negative. Did you feel more confident and effective? Did others treat you differently? This exercise can help us understand the impact of our appearance on our professional life and decide if we want to make any changes.

One final note for executives on this touchy subject. When it comes to the most important meeting of the month or quarter, the board of directors meeting, a business suit can be our suit of armor. Wearing a suit signifies your respect for the occasion and your readiness to engage seriously. It can give you the upper hand, projecting confidence and authority. Being appropriately dressed for business can also affect how you handle challenging situations. If a board member happens to ask, "Why the fancy suit?" it's a perfect time to remind them that their meeting is the most important meeting of the month.

THE GOOD LEADER

Temper Your Enthusiasm

Over the years, audience members have challenged me on my belief that enthusiasm is the number one and most important emotion. What about love? What about fear? My answer has always been, "What's love or fear without enthusiasm?" Love without enthusiasm for the other person seldom builds love and fear without enthusiasm suggests there's not much to fear. Enthusiasm will always be my number one emotion as it not only energizes others, but it also energizes me. Enthusiasm and energy are contagious and can significantly impact our effectiveness as a leader or manager. *(Secret)* Bringing zest to our work can inspire our team and create a positive, dynamic work environment.

While enthusiasm might seem overused, finding new ways to express and embody it can reinvigorate your approach to leadership. Embracing zest means approaching challenges with a positive attitude and a proactive mindset. This energy can drive innovation, motivate teams, and improve overall productivity. By maintaining a zestful approach, we can keep ourselves and our teams engaged and committed to achieving our goals.

CHAMBER WORLD

Enthusiasm is our presence and our influence. People are attracted to enthusiastic leaders and people are influenced by the enthusiasm of others. I can't imagine life or work without enthusiasm. I can also attest to enthusiasm for saving the dignity of my new board of directors and allowing me to take control in overcoming a twenty-thousand-dollar deficit I inherited on my first day.

I had won the nationwide search to be the new executive and was more than enthusiastic about my new job only to realize within two hours with our bookkeeper that the chamber was quickly going broke. In a nutshell, my new board had approved the former executive's recommendation to move into a new office. The location, location, location of the new office excited the board so much that they overlooked the price, the expenses and the cost of leasing and maintaining that office. It was now my job to tell the people who just hired me that they made a huge mistake.

And then it came to me; they were overcome by their own enthusiasm. I mean, who could be ashamed of that? Instead of finding fault, I found a solution to my predicament. I held an emergency meeting and started with these words, "Ladies and gentlemen, in approving the lease for our new building with its premier location, larger office space, and huge parking lot, *we became victims of our own enthusiasm.*" Notice that I said we and instead of bowing their heads in shame, they began nodding in agreement. They got caught up in the excitement, bit off more than they could chew, and fulfilled every other cliché defining the debacle. I just kept the focus on enthusiasm and redirected into moving forward.

It was one of our finest moments in working together. *(Secret)* Blaming is aiming in the wrong direction when confronting problems or crisis. Blaming will always waste our time while framing the issue in a positive light will always move us forward quickly.

I'm a great fan of Rotary Clubs and Rotary International. I began my civic involvement as student body president in High School when the local Lions Club made me an honorary member for a year as they did for all ASB presidents. I loved it. Service clubs, no matter the brand, are full of work hard, play hard people who care deeply about community. Within ten years of graduation, I found myself elected president of another Lions Club that ultimately led to my being recruited to the local chamber of commerce in The Dalles, Oregon.

Civic service clubs are where I learned to be passionate about organization visions and missions. The Lions Club[4] and Rotary Club[5] both had similar, yet simple and powerful mission statements. "We serve" has led the Lions Club for as long as I can remember and "Service Above Self" has directed Rotarians for over a century. I left the Lions Club when my Chamber career took me north to Lakewood, Washington where I became a Rotarian.

In The Dalles, the Lions Club was the dominant, or at least most visible civic organization. In Lakewood, it was Rotary. The Lakewood Rotary Club was a virtual "Who's Who" in the community south of Tacoma. It was tough leaving the Lions but ultimately the smart move as a chamber executive. I was surrounded by the smartest and most successful people you could imagine and grew exponentially as a young chamber executive. *(Secret)* Always join the dominant civic organization in the communities you serve, regardless of the name.

The Rotary Club also featured what I believe is the finest ethics test ever. It's called "The Four-Way Test" of the things we think, do, and say. Four powerful questions that begin with, is it, is it, and will it, will it.

---

[4] https://www.lionsclubs.org/en/footer/lions-press-center
[5] https://my.rotary.org/

THE GOOD LEADER

"Is it the truth? If not, we need not go any further.

Is it fair to all concerned? If not, we need to keep working and planning.

Will it build goodwill and better friendships? What could be a better outcome?

Will it be beneficial to all concerned? Who could be hurt by our actions?" [6]

Memorizing this little test so I wouldn't be fined at club meetings became much more valuable inside my *Chamber World*. One morning an excited member came running into the chamber office to drop off 1,200 advertising inserts for the mailing of our monthly newsletter. I happened to be the only one in the office when this chamber member, a fellow Rotarian dropped his stack on the reception desk. We were friends and colleagues, so I took a closer look to see what his business was up to. Oh, no.

To save everyone's dignity, I will paraphrase. The advertisement basically said, MY COMPANY IS THE BEST and then listed each of his competitors by name and sharing what each competitor was doing wrong. Many of those competitors were also members of the

---

[6] https://my.rotary.org/

chamber. Oh, no. The word that comes to mind was flummoxed. I was flummoxed. I had to tell him face-to-face there was no way I would include this advertisement in the next chamber mailing.

"Why not?" he said, in a very unhappy tone. This is where I was flummoxed, until I glanced at my office and saw a little plastic billboard on my desk featuring the Rotary Four-Way Test. Aha! I told him it doesn't pass the Four-Way Test and my reasoning was right in front of me. The conversation went something like this:

I asked him, "Is this stuff about your competitors really true?"

"Your damn right it's true! And I can prove it!" he replied excitedly.

"Well," I said, "It may be true, but it's definitely not fair to all concerned, especially to the chamber."

"Whaddya mean NOT FAIR?!" he said, still excited.

"First," I offered, "it's not fair to your competitors because they can't respond. Next, it's not fair to the chamber because you're asking us to endorse a campaign against

THE GOOD LEADER

seven other businesses, six of which are members and lastly, it's not fair to you."

Still excited with some nose flares, "Whaddya mean NOT FAIR TO ME?!"

"Look at it," I said with an unexcited and slight smile. "You are basically saying your industry is terrible by advertising that people can't trust $7/8^{ths}$ of the companies in your business. To me, that's unfair," and I followed with, "and there's no way this ad will build goodwill or better friendships, much less be beneficial to all concerned. We're not going to run it."

"That's it then. I quit! I'm out of the chamber!" he said, storming out the door.

The next morning, the phone rang exactly at 8:00 a.m. when we opened the chamber. You know who it was, and he was no longer huffing.

"Pat, I was up all-night thinking about it," he started.

"That makes two of us," I interrupted.

"Uh, Sorry about that. You were right and I'm totally wrong about this campaign and I'm not dropping the chamber. In fact, if you need support on anything, call my office."

I said, "Thanks, but I won't hold it against you. In our business, we call it being a victim of our own enthusiasm, and it happens to all of us."

Before hanging up he said, "Thanks, but there's one more thing; please avoid Northwest Boulevard. I'm ordering that they take down the billboard I had put up yesterday."

The Four-Way Test was also critical in justifying the change from the fair share due's structure that wasn't fair because it wasn't always truthful. The member driven tiered system allowing them access to select their level of support answered all the questions correctly. Thinking back, maybe our worlds didn't collide as much as they complemented one another.

The power of thought in shaping our actions and futures cannot be overstated. Being mindful of what we allow into our mind through what we see and hear can significantly influence our behavior and outcomes. Positive, constructive thinking leads to positive actions and habits, ultimately shaping a successful and fulfilling future. The choice is ours; we can align with winners or whiners.

THE GOOD LEADER

Monitoring and cultivating our thoughts involve being selective about the media we consume and the people we interact with. I'm never surprised when I hear someone say they never watch the news or that they've turned off social media. Surrounding myself with people who have a positive presence will influence me in how I choose to influence others. This practice can lead to a more intentional and mission-driven life.

Our Greatest Competition Is in The Mirror

In the age of social media, it's easy to fall into the trap of comparing our achievements with those of others. *(Secret)* However, a more productive approach is to compare yourself with yourself. Compare yourself to who you were yesterday, last week, and last year. This mindset shift allows us to focus and control our personal growth and continuous improvement rather than using external benchmarks where we have no control.

The greatest meeting room is one with a mirror. This isn't about checking our hair; it's about checking our eyes. If I can look at myself eye to eye without looking away, I find those are the times when I'm being honest with myself. The times when my eyes dip, look down or turn away, I'm usually justifying or rationalizing trying to make a wrong, right. I learned long ago the definition of rationalize is in the word itself; ration of lies. And when we rationalize, the first person we lie to is in the mirror.

Time Management

Of time and money, time is the greatest roadblock to professional and personal success. We can always make more money, but we are limited to 24 hours each day. We can make better use of our time, but we can't make more time.

When someone says, "I don't have time," what they are really saying is, "This isn't a priority," because, we all have the same amount of time in each day. The first step in how we can make our priorities their priorities is to fully respect their time when they are with us. If we do this well, they know we will respect their time by never wasting their time in chamber meetings or projects.

The first and highest respect for time is being on time! A great lesson learned in becoming a certified professional facilitator (CPF) was to ALWAYS start every meeting on time, or as my instructor put it... "Never punish the punctual." This simple and profound rule significantly impacted the efficiency, the professionalism, and the attendance of the meetings and events I facilitated.

(Secret) This little phrase should be shared at every volunteer and new member orientation to set an expected standard for efficient and effective meetings. "Never punish the punctual" should be our mantra for all meetings in *Chamber World*. Never punishing the punctual means, we will start without you and won't interrupt the discussion to catch you up.

Adopting this one discipline will lessen or possibly eliminate the "I don't have time" excuse because we have consistently proven our respect for everyone's time. Instead of time being a roadblock, let it become an expectation that we will never waste our volunteer's time.

The difference between time management and time leadership is segmentation. According to Covey[7], managers segment their time into the four categories of Urgent + Important / Not Urgent but Important / Urgent but not important, and / Not Urgent + Not Important, all of which takes additional

---

[7] Covey, Stephen R, The Seven Habits of Highly Effective People: Restoring the Character Ethic. New York, Simon and Schuster, 1989.

time. A leader has one category entitled *priorities*.

Don't Lead in a Vacuum

Effective communication is crucial in leadership. In my view, one word defines true communication, and that one word is understanding. Understand? If yes, we've communicated and if not understood, nothing has been communicated. We're wasting time. Leaders must ensure their messages are clear and that they genuinely understand the concerns and feedback from staff and members. This involves active listening and no-fault communication strategies where the focus is on responsibility rather than blame.

Emotional intelligence is having the capacity to be aware of and controlling how we express our emotions. Obviously, emotional intelligence is key to both our professional and personal successes. In *Chamber World*, our days are filled with happy, sad, mad, and glad emotions. How we portray these emotions plays a crucial role in navigating interpersonal dynamics while trying to create a culture of open and honest dialogue.

As leaders, it's our responsibility to get our messages across. This approach maintains a culture of open and honest dialogue, where staff members feel empowered to share their ideas and concerns.

For example, during board and staff orientations, we often assume that everyone understands the basics as well as we do. However, we sometimes get that 'deer in the headlights' expression from people we thought would easily grasp the training. What happened? Were they distracted, intimidated, or uncomfortable? It could be any of these reasons, but one thing for sure is that it wasn't anyone's fault. Recognizing these potential barriers to understanding can help us tailor our communication strategies to better meet the needs of every audience.

When a staff member disagrees with their executive, they should be comfortable in talking directly to the executive or to a higher-ranking staff member without fear or intimidation. I'm happy to say my teams always had the right to challenge my ideas without fear.

It was a time when our economy was rocking, the Chamber was growing, and I wanted more. So, I attended a seminar promoting "Guerrilla Marketing." The speaker was focusing on first impressions and shared a story about a company called Bob's Plumbing, that fired me up. This seminar not only provided valuable marketing insights but also reinforced the importance of staying ahead of industry trends and continuously seeking new ways with new knowledge. Again, if we don't try something new, we are guaranteed to be something old.

So powerful and so simple. Plumber Bob answered the phone with, "Bob's Plumbing, I can help you!" even before he knew what the problem was. He didn't say, "How can I help you?" or "Thank you for calling," he said he was ready to go to work for you right now. Bob was ready to help no matter what the problem was. It would be hard not to do business with Bob.

I could not wait to get back to the Chamber office. Implementing this kind of proactive customer service mindset would significantly expand the Chamber's mission of serving, protecting, and promoting our members and our community. All I could think about was every staff member answering the phone with, "Coeur d'Alene Chamber, I can help you!"

I went immediately to our front-line information director, Brenda, and said this was how we're going to answer the phone from now on. That's when I heard the words that taught me another great management lesson. She said, *Oh no, we're not.* This pushback highlighted the importance of involving team members in the decision-making process and to consider their perspectives before implementing changes.

"Wait a minute! I'm president and Chief Executive Officer and I say, yes, we are," then Brenda calmly replied, "Pat, what you're telling me is that you really don't know my job." She then went on to list the crazy questions people ask when they call the chamber of commerce that are unrelated to our work and she said, "That's why I can't help everyone that calls." She was tough to argue with, but deep down I knew between all of us we could help every caller at least get started in finding their answers.

This honest feedback underscored the importance of understanding the day-to-day challenges faced by front-line staff. That's when it came to me, how about this; let's answer the phone with, "Coeur d' Alene Chamber, *WE* can help you!" and anytime someone asks a crazy question, send it back to the corner office and give it to me."

"Oh," she said with a sly smile, "I can do that."

Coeur d'Alene Chamber, we can help you! was a great first impression when people called, and Brenda taught me to take the time to understand the real insights of every job in our chamber of commerce. Her brutal honesty was in essence, a compliment to a management style I tried to nurture every day.

Organization Management

Organization Management is a job with too many bosses, and the first rule in organization management is simple but almost always forgotten in the heat of the moment: *always put a volunteer between you and the problem.*

A common problem for many executives is getting a salary increase, so veteran executives will find a supportive volunteer to carry the torch, so the request doesn't appear mercenary or selfish.

When the problem is an unhappy member, finding a supportive volunteer to mitigate or facilitate a solution should always be the first rule for problem solving in the *Chamber World*. This approach not only protects the executive but also empowers volunteers, giving them a sense of responsibility and ownership in the organizations' success.

If we were ever to tattoo a rule on our arm, this would be the one. This first rule in organization management has been offered at the U.S. Chamber of Commerce Institute for

Organization Management since time immemorial. Why? Job security. Veteran executives know that face-to-face confrontation with the wrong person is job suicide, so get someone else to speak for you when you can.

However, there's also a downside. This rule can become problematic if misused. With thousands of chamber professionals not holding executive positions in their organization, the number one rule can become a number one problem for staff members, the volunteers, and the organization executive when a staff person uses the rule to go over the executive's head on an operational, or management issue. Misuse of this rule can lead to organization dysfunction and erode trust with all involved, highlighting the need for clear boundaries and ethical guidelines in its application.

If a staff member disagrees with their executive, they should talk directly to either the executive or higher-ranking staff member, but never a board member. If a staff member believes fraud or unethical behavior is taking place at the executive level, they should meet directly with the next person identified in the policy and procedure chain of authority, beginning with their department head, up to the chief operating officer level, or as a last step, the chairman of the board. Staff must never direct issues with random or friendly board members they might feel comfortable in telling. Never.

This ensures that issues are addressed through the proper channels, maintaining organization integrity and accountability. Putting a volunteer between you and the problem is an excellent concept except when it is abused and used for going over or around the person in charge. Then the rule is truly unfair to all involved. Understanding this rule should be a staff meeting agenda item for discussion and clarification every time a new staff member comes on board. Regular discussions about this rule can help reinforce its proper use and prevent potential misunderstandings or conflicts, ensuring that it serves its intended purpose of protecting the executive, and the staff.

Chapter Eight

Cultivating Excellence in Staff

CHAMBER WORLD

CULTIVATING EXCELLENCE IN STAFF

Employees put the direction of the chamber in motion, so managing and motivating them is key. Implementing strategies to recruit the best talent, retain them, and reward their efforts appropriately is vital for any organization's success. Recognizing and celebrating employee achievements, such as Employee of the Month events, can significantly boost morale and loyalty. Providing regular opportunities for professional development and ensuring a positive work environment can further employee satisfaction and performance.

Just out of college and eager to start a career in broadcasting, I worked as a grocery cashier in Portland, Oregon. It was a great job with a good and regular paycheck. However, my true aspiration was to break into broadcasting. While working as a grocery clerk, I landed my first major market break as the all-night DJ at KPAM-FM in Portland. The pay at KPAM-FM wasn't great, so I juggled both jobs, getting by on about five hours of sleep each day.

CHAMBER WORLD

Despite the exhaustion, I loved every minute of it. Then, everything changed when my estranged father called to tell me he was dying and wanted to reconcile. I left both jobs and drove to Newport Beach, California, the very next day. This pivotal moment taught me the importance of balancing passion with responsibility, and how personal sacrifices are sometimes necessary for greater personal growth.

After our reconciliation and my father's death, I returned to Portland hoping to get my radio job back, but it was no longer available. I went back to the grocery store and assured Ed Murphy, the store manager, that I was committed to building a career there. Without hesitation, he put me back to work.

The following morning, while checking out customers, I received a call from KOOL-FM radio in Phoenix, Arizona, offering me a job. I was torn because I had just promised Ed I was back for good. When I told Ed about the offer, he said, "Pat, it's a GROCERY STORE. Get out of here and go to Phoenix!" His words were a revelation. This experience underscored the value of having a mentor-employer who can see beyond immediate commitments to the bigger picture, and the importance of pursuing opportunities that align with one's true aspirations.

CULTIVATING EXCELLENCE IN STAFF

As I drove to Phoenix, I vowed to manage people the way Ed Murphy did, always putting their interests and careers first. This philosophy proved successful. When my teams knew I would sacrifice for their future, they would, in turn, sacrifice for me in the present. *(Secret)* This mutual commitment proved once again that you get what you give. This approach became a cornerstone of my leadership and management style, ensuring that my teams always felt as loyal to me as I was to them.

Today, more than ever, recruiting, retaining, and rewarding employees are at the top of every employer's list. And therefore, finding ways to support our members with their staff issues should be a priority for all of us in the *Chamber World*. We all know that a Ribbon Cutting is a great one-time benefit in helping new members get new business. But what about the other eleven months?

The concept of holding a monthly employee-of-the-month breakfast for our members to publicly recognize their employees of the month would raise the recognition much higher and encourage more employees to strive for the award.

The only problem I can envision is being sold out and doing the extra work to pre-book members into future breakfasts. At the very least, invite members to bring their employees of the month to our regular monthly meetings to be invited to stand and be applauded.

Taking Care of Our People

Human resource management is a vital aspect of leadership inside our *Chamber Worlds*. This involves not only managing employees but also volunteers. Ensuring that our teams feel valued, motivated, and safe will enhance their productivity and commitment to the chamber of commerce. Regular feedback, encouragement, professional development opportunities, and a supportive work environment are key components of effective human resource management and leadership. The first step in taking care of people is to begin with genuinely caring about them.

Creating an established culture of employee success is essential even if it means losing great employees to career goals of their own. Oddly, I found through the years that pushing people to attain their dreams would make them want to stay. One of the first questions I would ask while interviewing people for any position was, "Do you have a Goal Job?" If they didn't have an answer, I didn't have a job for them. I was always looking for people who had higher goals. The chamber is an outstanding steppingstone in reaching any goal job. If any applicant responded with a yes and I hired them, I would offer to help and support them in getting that goal job when it became available.

This was a wonderful offer, but it came with two caveats. First, they would have to work as hard as I worked every day and that meant if I had a down day, they could too. They just had to guess which day it would be, (which was never.) Next, I asked for a handshake agreement with them giving me 30 days' notice instead of the standard two weeks' notice when leaving a job. I wanted this for a couple reasons and told them why. I needed two weeks for them to help me find someone just like them, and two weeks for them to train the new person as they knew the job far better than I did.

In exchange, they would never have to fear me knowing they were looking for a better job and I would gladly offer a letter of recommendation if they lived up to my caveats. That letter of recommendation motivated them to work as if their next job depended on it and the lack of fear of looking for another job built a trusting environment most weren't in a rush to leave. I call it my Push/Pull Theory; when we push people away, they pull back and when we pull people in trying to keep them, they push away. It wasn't meant to be reverse psychology; it was meant to show that I cared about them.

(Secret) Encourage your team to pursue their goals, new opportunities for growth and development and to build their resume with successes from their work in the chamber.

If it's to be, it's NOT up to me.

As a leader our role is to guide, inspire, and empower our teams, not to do their work for them. Delegating tasks and trusting team members to execute them is crucial for building a high-performing organization. Thinking I'm the only one who can do this or that job will undermine any team's confidence and effectiveness, while trust in delegating will build our teams and their accountability.

I was a terrible delegator. I lived by the old cliché, *if it is to be, it is up to me.* Then a mentor's metaphor and an epiphany came to me.

Most mentors seem to be older instead of younger than us, but that's not always true. My chairman of the board at the time was the general manager of a major hotel and resort. He was five years my junior while years ahead of me in wisdom. Here I was, Chief Executive Officer of the Chamber, and he would see me

CULTIVATING EXCELLENCE IN STAFF

running around as if my head was cut off doing work that wasn't even close to being in my job description. It was then he called me into his office.

"Pat, how many beds do you think we have in this hotel?" I had no idea where this was going but I knew the hotel had over 300 rooms, some with two beds so I made an educated guess and answered, "I'd say around 400 beds." He said, "Close enough. Now let me ask you how many of those beds do you think I go up and make every morning?" I was starting to get a picture of where he was going. I said, "I don't think you go up and make any of them." And he said "EXACTLY! Making beds is not my job. My job is to guide and inspire a team of the hardest working people I know to take on that duty." He went on to say he had a dynamic team up there and if he went up there wanting to be a good guy and help out, his team wouldn't say thank you, instead they would feel he didn't trust them to do the work."

Furthermore, he asked, "What do you think the hotel owner would say if he saw his general manager upstairs making beds?" I knew the answer because I knew the owner. "I think he would say you're a pretty expensive bed maker." He said I was right again, and then told me, "Pat, you're a bed maker." He told me the Chamber didn't hire me to do staff or committee work, they hired me to guide, lead, and inspire people to fulfill their job descriptions, not do it for them.

That evening, I had an epiphany born from the bed maker meeting; how did our world ever get this far before I was born? How could they have done it WITHOUT Pat McGaughey? Then I thought, how can the world go on when I die? The answers to both questions were obvious of course. The realization of my real value, and ultimately, my real legacy was to lead well and leave this place better than I found it. To do that, was to teach, train, and inspire people to do their job.

A special note about bed makers and housekeepers in every hospitality property. They are the true marketing department. Their performance determines whether you and I will ever return. Their performance determines the status of their leadership and therefore, their performance determines the livelihoods of all who surround them. Never forget to tip housekeeping.

The Secret to Motivating Others

The EX.L.A.R.G.E. agenda discussed in the Vision to Vitality section goes far beyond planning sessions. Gail and I have used it in addressing personal and family issues

CULTIVATING EXCELLENCE IN STAFF

throughout our marriage long before creating the acronym. After being engaged and just weeks before our marriage she came to me and said, "Before we do this, you need to know something," she had my full attention. "After we're married and when we buy our first house, you need to know that we WILL park our cars in the garage, not on the driveway."

What? All men know that the garage is for STUFF, not for cars, but something told me this was no joke to her, and I agreed. For every year since, our garage has been used for parking our cars, not our stuff. The walls might look a little crazy, but the garage floor is reserved for our cars. *(Secret)* Expectations motivate other people.

Sharing this expectation with me in the beginning, along with a few other of her pet peeves saved hours, days, months or even years of frustration and aggravation for her. Those frustrations and aggravations could have grown like a cancer in our relationship, but she prevented it by sharing her expectations.

I never would have parked my car in the garage had she not told me how cars in the driveway bothered her so much. Loving her equally as much, *motivated* me to keep every garage clear of stuff for parking our cars.

CHAMBER WORLD

(Secret) Fulfill the expectations of others by sharing them. It's a silly story with serious meaning.

If I know your expectations and you know mine, we have something to build upon. Without these expectations we have nothing to go on and hence there is no motivation.

For The Success of Others

When I reflect on my career in the *Chamber World*, those five words "For the success of others" define the purpose that drove me and all who surrounded me toward success. For the success of others. It's another way to define the Golden Rule, just as the First Rule in Business which states, "You get what you give." It's a rule, yes, and we all know that rules are meant to be broken, but hopefully, not by us.

The best teams are those that can repeat their success and build a lasting legacy. As a chamber leader, it's crucial to maintain momentum especially after significant achievements. Setting new goals, celebrating successes, and always striving for improvement should be at the core of our leadership philosophy. One of my mantras, "If you're coasting, you have to be going downhill," was essential in sustaining our

CULTIVATING EXCELLENCE IN STAFF

long-term success, no matter the economic conditions.

This relentless pursuit of success and excellence can inspire our teams to continuously seek out new challenges and opportunities for growth. Not because they have to, but because they want to. This attitude builds respect among peers and is fundamental for any organization seeking success.

Promoting punctuality and respect for others' time during meetings are small concepts with huge results. Relentlessly setting a professional tone ensures efficient and effective operations for our own success which then supports our efforts ensuring the success of others. When we can multiply the value of this thinking inside all *Chamber Worlds*, our position in every community can only grow stronger.

About the Author

Patrick H. McGaughey, CPF, IOM, is an international speaker, business consultant and certified professional facilitator. Pat's professional career began in broadcasting as an on-air personality which evolved into sales and management positions that led to the chamber of commerce industry. Pat served three chambers of commerce in the Pacific Northwest rebuilding three failing organizations.

His success in Coeur d'Alene gave Pat a national reputation for membership growth, non-dues income and for volunteer development. In 1994, Pat developed and introduced the first tiered dues program in the nation and from 2000 to 2019, Pat was a regular faculty member for the United States Chamber of Commerce Institute for Organization Management where he regularly receives the highest possible classroom evaluations for content and presentation.

Pat and his wife Gail, a former Executive Director for the local United Way, live in the beautiful resort community of Coeur d'Alene, Idaho where they have two grown children, five grandchildren and a fishing boat always geared and ready for beautiful Lake Coeur d'Alene.

Email: pat@chambermentor.com

www.ingramcontent.com/pod-product-compliance
Lightning Source LLC
Chambersburg PA
CBHW071826210526
45479CB00001B/14